OUTCOME

A BLUEPRINT
For Becoming
an
Effective Church

TIM PASSMORE

CREATION
H O U S E
A STRANG COMPANY

OUTCOME: A BLUEPRINT FOR BECOMING AN EFFECTIVE
CHURCH by Tim Passmore
Published by Creation House
A Strang Company
600 Rinehart Road
Lake Mary, Florida 32746
www.creationhouse.com

This book or parts thereof may not be reproduced in any
form, stored in a retrieval system, or transmitted in any form
by any means—electronic, mechanical, photocopy, recording, or otherwise—without prior written permission of the
publisher, except as provided by United States of America
copyright law.

Unless otherwise noted, all Scripture quotations are from the
Holy Bible, New International Version. Copyright © 1973,
1978, 1984, International Bible Society. Used by permission.

Scripture quotations marked NLT are from the Holy Bible,
New Living Translation, copyright © 1996. Used by permis-
sion of Tyndale House Publishers, Inc., Wheaton, IL 60189.
All rights reserved.

Cover design by Terry Clifton

Copyright © 2006 by Tim Passmore
All rights reserved

Library of Congress Control Number: 2005936908
International Standard Book Number: 1-59185-983-2

First Edition

06 07 08 09— 987654321
Printed in the United States of America

CONTENTS

PREFACE

The lessons I share in this book have become very real to me over the past several years. They are not a collection of ideas that might work; they are truths that do work. They have been proven effective in producing God-sized outcomes, results that can only be explained by His involvement.

When I arrived as pastor at Woodland, I really thought I knew how to lead a church. After all, I had a seminary degree! If that wasn't enough, I was the son of a pastor who was instrumental in growing a dynamic and evangelistic church. I had served as a staff member under an incredible pastor in a large church that was serious about reaching its community. I had even been successful in leading a growing student ministry.

Although I had this strong background, I learned very quickly that the life of a pastor is quite different than the life of a youth minister. I immediately began to deal with staff issues and ministries aimed at age groups I was not accustomed to serving. I was responsible to set the course for the entire church and make sure that all the ministries worked together to accomplish a common purpose. Volunteer leaders who oversaw ministries needed direction. The church budget needed attention so we could have the needed resources to perform ministry. And I also faced the challenge of leading a congregation in an area that was changing drastically from a rural to suburban culture.

I realized that I must address the many components that affect the outcome of the church. It was not enough to just preach a strong message on what believers are to do. The church needed a plan and an environment that encouraged cooperation. Everyone in the church needed a proper understanding of what God wanted us to do. I learned that the believers who compose the church must have the correct passion for God to accomplish His plan. We would have no significant results unless we addressed these areas of concern.

All these pressures overwhelmed me, and I turned to God to understand His will for the church. I recognized that the church is an organization and that the leader must address issues that affect its organizational health if it is to accomplish its goals. I discovered that the Bible has much to say about the organizational concerns of the church. Through the study of His Word and the leadership of His Spirit, God gave me a biblical blueprint for the ministry of the church. God has used this blueprint to keep the focus of our church on the areas that determine its success. The results have been amazing, and the outcome we have experienced can only be explained by the involvement of God. I believe that God can also use this blueprint to help your church experience a God-sized outcome as you build a church of servants.

I have written this book for three groups of people. First, I speak to the staff members of the local church. The church staff must cast a vision that is centered on the purposes of the church. It must develop a plan of ministry to accomplish the vision and have a way to measure its progress. Finally, it must hold members accountable for accomplishing the purposes of the church.

Many staff members become frustrated as they lead volunteers within the church. They have a true passion to reach, develop, and involve others in ministry but do not know how to do it. I have good news for you. The blueprint you learn in this book will keep you on task so you can experience these results. You will learn about the critical components that affect church organization. You will also learn a plan that will help you organize your ministries and your volunteer leaders, measure the success of your ministries, and monitor the development of your members in growth toward servanthood.

This book is also written for volunteer leaders within the church. Leaders must be aware of the purposes of the church and the ministry plan used to fulfill these purposes. They must understand the role of their particular ministry in the process of leading a non-believer to the point of salvation and leading a new believer to become involved in ministry. They must also learn that their ministry is an organization and its health depends on the ministry leader giving proper attention to issues that affect organizational life.

Finally, servants within the church will benefit from this book. A servant participates as a functioning part of the body of Christ. Each servant must grasp how personal ministry affects the body and how he can properly function within the body to bring about God-sized results.

I'm praying for you! My passion is to help you become a dynamic, community-changing church that brings glory to God. I encourage you to take time right now and ask God to reveal to you His plan for His church. Remember, it's not your church! It's His church. Let's give His church the attention it deserves by learning about His plan of ministry—to work together as His body to change the world.

The construction project begins.

INTRODUCTION

For it is by grace you have been saved, through faith—and this not from yourselves, it is the gift of God—not by works, so that no one can boast. For we are God's workmanship, created in Christ Jesus to do good works, which God prepared in advance for us to do.

—EPHESIANS 2:8–10

Will it hit us? Many residents in our area were asking this question as the weather experts continually forecasted the landfall of Hurricane Charley. My children had never experienced a hurricane before and were actually excited about the event. This may sound morbid, especially when you understand the destructive nature of a category-four storm. They weren't excited about the hurricane itself; the hurricane merely allowed them to have a day off from school.

I did not share the enthusiasm of my children. I remember growing up on the Gulf Coast of Florida and experiencing hurricanes during my childhood. I saw the evidence of their destructive power. Who can forget the images shown on our television screens after hurricanes Hugo and Andrew? I still remember the pictures of homes that were reduced to piles of rubble by the storms.

Great advances in technology help forecast hurricanes today. My wife and I watched a telecast hosted by local newscasters as they began to notice on radar that the storm was turning. It moved toward the east, directly into Charlotte Harbor, approximately fifty miles south of our home. Our community was spared, but unfortunately the city of Punta Gorda was not. Many houses in that area looked as if someone had plowed through them on a bull dozer, with no regard for the possessions that lay within their walls.

Thousands of homes were declared uninhabitable by the Federal Emergency Management Agency, while others survived the winds and rain with very little damage. Why did they survive? Those who have lived in Florida for some time know that the hurricane building codes have changed over the years. More recently, the construction of homes has followed a building plan that produces a structure that can withstand the force of a violent storm.

The hurricane seasons of 2004 and 2005 have brought new life to one of Jesus' parables. He said:

> Therefore everyone who hears these words of mine and puts them into practice is like a wise man who built his house on the rock. The rain came down, the streams rose, and the winds blew and beat against that house; yet it did not fall, because it had its foundation on the rock. But everyone who hears these words of mine and does not put them into practice is like a foolish man who built his house on sand. The rain came down, the streams rose, and the winds blew and beat against that house, and it fell with a great crash.
>
> —MATTHEW 7:24–27

"Crashed" homes are not pretty sights. Seeing them motivates those who live in high risk areas to prepare for the storms that may one day come. Jesus gave this parable to illustrate our lives and what we build our lives upon. "Crashed" lives are also tragic.

How does this relate to the church? The last time I checked, people make up the church. Their spiritual strength and their willingness to be God's servants determine the effectiveness of the church. God uses servants within the church to bring about God-sized results. Our desire should be to produce believers who use their gifts in ministry to affect the world.

Jesus gave us an example of the type of person He wants to build His church upon when He said to Peter, "And I tell you that you are Peter, and on this rock I will build my church, and the gates of Hades will not overcome it" (Matt. 16:18). Jesus found someone who would not buckle under pressure while building the church. He recognized the importance of Peter's influence in directing the church to fulfill God's purposes. Peter was successful because of his "rock solid" spiritual strength maintained out of a passion for God and his service within the body of Christ. Peter was willing to make the sacrifices that were necessary to advance the kingdom of God. He had a "whatever it takes" attitude.

The health of the church today is also dependent upon leaders and members who have "rock solid" spiritual strength and live out their passion for God by performing acts of service. This must also be done with a "whatever it takes" attitude. Satan deliberately brings pressure against the church to stop the message of Christ. He wants the church to come crashing down, and he accomplishes this by influencing us to serve someone other than God. He knows that we will no longer serve people when we no longer serve God. This is the temptation he brings against us.

Satan tempted Jesus in this way. The Scriptures tell us:

> Again, the devil took him to a very high mountain and showed him all the kingdoms of the world and their splendor. "All this I will give you," he said, "if you will bow down and worship me." Jesus said to him, "Away

from me, Satan! For it is written: 'Worship the Lord your God, and serve him only.'"

—Matthew 4:8–10

We are to serve God alone. Satan wants us to serve someone other than God because this brings glory to someone other than Him. This is sin.

Paul wrote, "For all have sinned and fall short of the glory of God" (Rom. 3:23). Satan loves it when we live to bring glory to ourselves. Selfish people are our adversary's biggest weapon against the church. Why? Selfish people don't serve other people; they serve themselves. As long as we are serving ourselves, we will not spread the message of God's love to those around us. If a church is composed of people who turn inward, it will crumble and fall. However, if a church is composed of people who maintain their concern for others and prove their concern by being agents of God's love, it will grow in strength and change our world. "Rock solid" servants are God's biggest weapon against His enemy.

We are to bring glory to God. Paul instructed the church of Corinth, "So whether you eat or drink or whatever you do, do it all for the glory of God" (1 Cor. 10:31). Jesus is our example of how we are to bring glory to God. He taught that our greatness is defined by our service. He said, "Whoever wants to become great among you must be your servant, and whoever wants to be first must be your slave—just as the Son of Man did not come to be served, but to serve, and to give his life as a ransom for many" (Matt. 20:26–28). Jesus' purpose was to serve others, not to be served. We are the body of Christ; therefore, our purpose is also to serve others. The moment members within the body begin to care more about being served than being servants is the moment that the church begins to lose its effectiveness.

Salvation is not the end of God's plan for us, it is the beginning. Paul wrote to the church at Ephesus: "For it is by grace you have been saved, through faith—and this not from yourselves, it is the gift of God—not by works, so that no one can boast" (Eph. 2:8–9). This verse teaches us some important truths. First, we learn that we are saved through faith and faith alone. We cannot earn our way to heaven. Second, we learn how we come to place our faith in God. We place our faith in God because of His grace. God reveals His love through His grace. He shows His love to us even though we don't deserve it. His love is seen through the sacrifice of His Son, Jesus, who died for us upon the cross. God's grace changes our hearts. Just as we can see God's grace through His love shown to us through Jesus, others can see God's grace through our acts of love and our actions of sacrifice. These actions are called acts of service.

I have quoted Ephesians 2:8–9 many times as I have shared Christ with those who are lost. After all, it is by grace that we are saved. However, we do a disservice to people when we do not quote the next verse in this passage. Ephesians 2:10 says, "For we are God's workmanship, created in Christ Jesus to do good works, which God prepared in advance for us to do." This scripture tells us why we are saved: we are saved to serve. We are created in Christ to do work that He has already prepared for us. Unfortunately, many are missing out on the joy that comes when we live up to the reason for our spiritual birth—serving God with love.

Church leaders need to think of themselves as builders. Paul taught this to the church at Ephesus. He wrote: "It was he who gave some to be apostles, some to be prophets, some to be evangelists, and some to be pastors and teachers, to prepare God's people for works of service, so that the body of Christ may be built up until we all reach unity in the faith and in the knowledge of the Son of God and become mature, attaining to the whole measure of the fullness of Christ" (Eph. 4:11–13). The pastors and teachers are not to do the work of the church; they are to prepare the people within the church to do God's work.

This book is written to help leaders and members of the local body of Christ construct churches that are effective and that can stand and make a difference. We are pursuing a very specific outcome—to reach the lost with the good news of Christ, help new believers grow in their faith, and involve maturing believers in ministry as servants of God. A church that succeeds in developing servants of God experiences worship that is more vibrant, better fellowship, more success in reaching the lost for Christ, and a discipleship ministry that is more effective in leading others to live a life of purity. Why? The answer is simple! Servants of God have a passion for God, and having a passion for God produces these results. It's called "cause and effect." Our love for God has a direct effect on our behavior. Church health is maintained when we love God together.

Constructing this type of church requires a building plan that will help us accomplish the result God desires—a church composed of people who are living out their predetermined purpose. The church is successful at reaching the lost, building believers, and involving people as servants when it uses a biblical plan of ministry as a blueprint for construction.

We will focus on many issues as we develop this building plan for the church. These issues will form the framework for the construction process. Each one gives the church stability and must be present for the church to succeed. If an element of the framework is missing or is weak, it changes the outcome of the ministry of the church.

By way of illustration, foundational posts hold up a beach home along the ocean. If one post is removed, the home is weakened. In the same way, if an element of the framework is removed from the church, its strength is compromised. The results of the ministry of the church are affected in a negative way. An area of vulnerability exists and can be attacked by Satan, causing the church to "crash." These elements become diagnostic tools to discover areas of weakness within the church. Leaders and members must address these areas of concern to bring about healing and good church health.

The Blueprint for Becoming an Effective Church

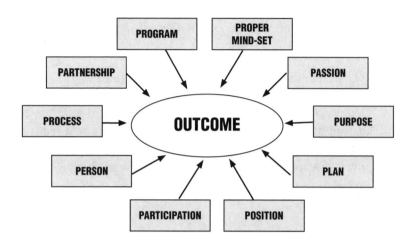

The foundational posts for constructing the church—topics that we will address in the contents of this book—are illustrated in the above diagram, which reveals that those who follow the blueprint:

    a. Have a *proper mind-set* concerning the characteristics of a healthy church;

    b. Operate the ministries of the church out of a *passion for God*;

    c. Understand their *purpose*;

    d. Develop a *plan of ministry* to accomplish God's purposes;

    e. Determine the spiritual *position* of people who are associated with the church;

    f. Define how leaders will *participate*;

g. Train each *person* to be effective in their role;

h. Have a *process of clear communication*;

i. Have leaders who *partner* together with others as a team;

j. Develop a *program of ministry* that will bring glory to God.

Do you have your construction clothes on? Are you ready to follow God's plan for ministry? Join me on this journey and discover how to participate in a church that can change your community and your world.

1

THE PROPER MIND-SET

You, my brothers, were called to be free. But do not use your freedom to indulge the sinful nature; rather, serve one another in love.

—GALATIANS 5:13

Determining the Characteristics of a Healthy Church

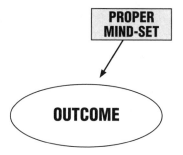

How do you define a healthy church? What is your mind-set on how to measure the health of the church? If we would ask several church leaders these questions, they would undoubtedly express many different ideas. Our responses to these questions are crucial because our beliefs about the health of the church have a direct bearing on the ministries we perform. Leaders tend to conduct activities that help them meet their definition of a healthy church.

We live in a society where the word *health* is used quite frequently. The term is applied to the condition of many things, and one of the best examples is our body. Scientists are working diligently to discover vaccines for diseases. New nutritional programs are being offered at a rapid pace, making promises of fast weight loss or higher energy. So what do we know about the health of the body? We know the parts that make up the body must function properly for the body to experience health. We also know that the body must maintain the right balance to be healthy. For example, the body begins to break down if its blood flow is restricted. We know that the body begins to deteriorate if too few cells are being produced.

What does this have to do with the health of the church? Let's define some terms to help us answer this question. First, we focus on the word *church*. The church is defined as "the body of Christ." The apostle Paul wrote: "Now you are the body of Christ, and each one of you is a part of it" (1 Cor. 12:27). Second, we focus on the word *health*, which means "freedom from disease."[1] A body that is free from disease functions in the proper manner. We combine these definitions and learn that a healthy church is defined as "the body of Christ properly functioning as Christ's body." Just as the physical body operates properly because of the continuing function of its parts and the balance it maintains, the church operates properly because its members fulfill their functions, and the ministries of the body maintain their balance.

THE CHURCH IS
TO FUNCTION AS THE BODY OF CHRIST

Christ, in His earthly body, served God. This was His purpose. He served God by revealing God's love through His ministry to others. He accomplished this task because He maintained proper spiritual health. We are a healthy church when we serve God. We also serve God by revealing His love through our ministry to others. After all, we are created in Christ Jesus for this purpose. Paul taught the church of Ephesus this truth when he wrote: "For we are God's workmanship, created in Christ Jesus to do good works, which God prepared in advance for us to do" (Eph. 2:10). We are saved to serve.

A healthy church is composed of members who fulfill their calling in ministry by serving others. Accomplishing this goal is evidence of our spiritual health. Paul gave evidence of his spiritual health through his passion for serving God. He wrote: "But my life is worth nothing unless I use it for doing the work assigned me by the Lord Jesus—the work of telling others the Good News about God's wonderful kindness and love." (Acts 20:24, NLT).

Jesus taught that people will know us by our fruit. He said:

> I am the vine; you are the branches. If a man remains in me and I in him, he will bear much fruit; apart from me you can do nothing. If anyone does not remain in me, he is like a branch that is thrown away and withers; such branches are picked up, thrown into the fire and burned. If you remain in me and my words remain in you, ask whatever you wish, and it will be given you. This is to my Father's glory, that you bear much fruit, showing your-selves to be my disciples.
> —JOHN 15:5–8

Jesus' teaching is very clear. We are to bear fruit. The reason for this is that those who bear fruit bring glory to God and prove that they are disciples of Christ. The fruit of our lives is the evidence used to diagnose our spiritual condition. The healthy church is composed of believers who bring glory to God by bearing fruits of service as disciples of Christ. This pleases the Lord. Paul instructed the church at Colosse about this:

> And we pray this in order that you may live a life worthy of the Lord and may please him in every way: bearing fruit in every good work, growing in the knowledge of God, being strengthened with all power according to his glorious might so that you may have great endurance and patience, and joyfully giving thanks to the Father, who has qualified you to share in the inheritance of the saints in the kingdom of light.[2]
>
> —COLOSSIANS 1:10–12

According to Paul, we please God when we bear fruit by doing good works. The more we grow in our knowledge of God and are strengthened by Him, the more we desire to serve Him.

Jesus was spiritually healthy, and He was unique in two ways. First, He was able to succeed spiritually in His physical body because of His pure heart. He trusted in God completely. No sin distracted Him away from His purpose of reaching out sacrificially through actions of love. Second, Jesus possessed the spiritual gifts required to meet the needs of every person. Not only did He possess these gifts, but He also exercised them. He was spiritually healthy because He maintained a spiritual exercise program called servanthood.

Believers are also spiritually healthy for the same reasons. First, we maintain our spiritual health by keeping our hearts pure, a condition that occurs when we trust in God completely. A pure heart fosters within a person the willingness to do what is necessary to meet needs. An impure heart contains elements of self-centeredness, a condition that reduces a person's willingness to make sacrifices. A heart that is fully devoted to God begins to change a person's behavior. God's Spirit directs this person completely, and he or she begins to live a life of "love, joy, peace, patience, kindness, goodness, faithfulness, gentleness and self-control" (Gal. 5:22–23).

Second, we maintain our spiritual health by participating in the spiritual exercise program called servanthood. We begin to use our spiritual gifts in acts of ministry.

Jesus is quite different from the rest of humanity. He was spiritually gifted in every area to meet every need. However, we are not, and we need one another. We must work as a team to operate as the body of Christ. The apostle Paul taught this:

> Now the body is not made up of one part but of many. If the foot should say, "Because I am not a hand, I do not belong to the body," it would not for that reason cease to be part of the body. And if the ear should say, "Because I am not an eye, I do not belong to the body," it would not for that reason cease to be part of the body. If the whole body were an eye, where would the sense of hearing be? If the whole body were an ear, where would the sense of smell be? But in fact God has arranged the parts in the body, every one of them, just as he wanted them to be. If they were all one part, where would the body be? As it is, there are many parts, but one body. The eye cannot say to the hand, "I don't need you!" And the head cannot say to the feet, "I don't need you!" On the contrary, those parts of the body that seem to be weaker are indispensable, and the parts that we think are less honorable we treat with special honor. And the parts that are unpresentable are treated with special modesty, while our presentable parts need no special treatment. But God has combined the members of the body and has given greater honor to the parts that lacked it, so that there should be no division in the body, but that its parts should have equal concern for each other. If one part suffers, every part suffers with it; if one part is honored, every part rejoices with it. Now you are the body of Christ, and each one of you is a part of it.
> —1 CORINTHIANS 12:14–27

Paul explained that all must fulfill their unique roles if we are to function as the body of Christ. The health of the church depends on it. Paul wrote:

> Just as each of us has one body with many members,
> and these members do not all have the same function,
> so in Christ we who are many form one body, and each
> member belongs to all the others. We have different gifts,
> according to the grace given us. If a man's gift is proph-
> esying, let him use it in proportion to his faith. If it is
> serving, let him serve; if it is teaching, let him teach; if it
> is encouraging, let him encourage; if it is contributing to
> the needs of others, let him give generously; if it is lead-
> ership, let him govern diligently; if it is showing mercy,
> let him do it cheerfully.
>
> —ROMANS 12:4–8

How do the members of your church measure the spiritual health of the people within the church? When I was growing up, I heard preachers say—half joking and half serious—that the *Christians* come to Sunday morning worship and the *committed Christians* come to Sunday morning worship and the Sunday evening service. And, they would conclude, *those who really love Jesus* come to church on Sunday morning and Sunday night and for the Wednesday night prayer service.

This may sound like a good way to measure our spiritual health. However, I must confess that I've known some people who really love Jesus who don't make it to all three services. How do I know they love Jesus? They prove their love for Christ by bearing fruit that brings glory to God. They are fulfilling their role in the body with a heart that is fully devoted to God. Believers are able to accomplish this by maintaining their spiritual health through the appropriate time spent with God. This is the correct measurement.

Philip Yancey and Dr. Paul Brand addressed the health of the church in their book *In the Likeness of God.* They compared the church as the body of Christ to the cells in the human body. Dr. Brand wrote, "I sometimes think of the human body as a community, and then of its individual cells such as the white cell. The cell is the basic unit of an organism; it can live for itself, or it can help form and sustain the larger organism."[2] He went on to say that a cell "can be part of the body as a loyalist, or it can cling to its own life. Some cells do choose to live in the body, sharing its benefits while maintaining complete independence—they become parasites or cancer cells."[3]

With this teaching, Dr. Brand showed that we can live for ourselves or for others and that our decision affects the body. Cells that do not live for other cells in the body become cancer cells, and cancer cells cause the body to become unhealthy. The same is true in the body of Christ. If we begin living for ourselves and not for others, we become cancerous and cause the church to become unhealthy. He emphasized the impact that cells have on the community atmosphere of the body.

> In exchange for its self-sacrifice, the individual cell can share in what I call the ecstasy of community. No scientist can yet measure how a sense of security or pleasure is communicated to the cells of the body, but individual cells certainly participate in our emotional reactions.... If you look for a pleasure nerve in the human body, you will come away disappointed; there is none. There are nerves for pain and cold and heat and touch, but no nerve gives a sensation of pleasure. Pleasure appears as a by-product of cooperation by many cells.[4]

Dr. Brand used the cells in the body to illustrate that we actually experience pleasure when we fulfill our roles in community. Pleasure in the body occurs as a by-product of cooperation and service. The same is true in the church, the body of Christ. Church life is to be a pleasurable experience. To ensure this outcome, a proper ministry balance must be maintained within the church. The balance of ministry is in place to assist the body of Christ as it reaches out to non-believers, develops new believers, and involves Christians in a life of service that God has prepared in advance for them.

The Healthy Church
Is a Balanced Church

Diet and nutrition are hot topics in our modern-day culture. Experts in nutrition advise us to have a balanced diet. Individuals who maintain this type of diet consume vitamins and nutrients that are needed to ward off harmful diseases and illnesses. The church is also in a position to maintain good health when it maintains proper balance in the area of ministries.

The balanced church does not focus on one area of ministry alone. Many churches lose their balance and become spiritually ill. For example, a church that concentrates on evangelism alone can become an unhealthy church. This may seem hard to believe since evangelism is the beginning point of ministry. After all, people cannot be discipled unless they are first saved.

However, if the church does not provide an effective plan of discipleship, many who make a commitment to Christ leave the church and may even become confused about their relationship with God. A church in this condition becomes a revolving door of ministry. Although new people come into the church, others are leaving at the same time. This problem actually limits the church's ability to become more evangelistic. Churches increase in evangelistic effectiveness when their members become spiritually mature and begin to exercise their faith as servants.

A strong discipleship ministry will deepen our love for God, and this in turn will deepen our love for others. Loving others is the key to evangelism. Paul said, "We loved you so much that we were delighted to share with you not only the gospel of God but our lives as well, because you had become so dear to us" (1 Thess. 2:8). The more we love others, the more we share the gospel. Believers who use their spiritual gifts in acts of service reveal God's love and have increased opportunities to share the good news of Jesus. The more servants a church develops the more evangelistic it becomes.

All believers have the responsibility to share their faith. This is not meant to be a burden. In fact, if sharing our faith is a burden, it reveals a spiritual sickness. We have become spiritually dehydrated and are no longer filled with God's Spirit. The spirit-filled believer automatically shares God's love with the lost. The Bible tells us what happened in the early church. "After they prayed, the place where they were meeting was shaken. And they were all filled with the Holy Spirit and spoke the word of God boldly" (Acts 4:31). This teaches us that we speak the Word of God boldly when God's Spirit fills us. Therefore, the way to become a more evangelistic church is to develop more spirit-filled believers.

We can't help speaking about Jesus when we are full of God's Spirit. Do you remember what Peter and John said? They spoke the following words to the religious officials who had commanded them not to speak for Jesus: "For we cannot help speaking about what we have seen and heard" (Acts 4:20). They could not help telling people about their encounter with Christ. Spirit-filled believers go beyond using their spiritual gifts in acts of service; they also share their story of how they came to know Jesus personally. Satan knows that sin keeps us from sharing our story. When sin seeps in, the Spirit of God is quenched and we stop speaking the good news. We allow something to become more important to us than God and begin bringing glory to someone other than Him. (See Romans 3:23.) Sin is the weapon Satan uses against us to silence the message of Christ.

Let's learn more about the balanced church. A church that focuses only on discipleship can also become an unhealthy church. The church with this concentration has a tendency to become very self-centered. Individuals begin to believe that spiritual success is measured by the amount of factual knowledge gained and not by the servant activities that are performed. Members come to church only to gain knowledge and do not serve those who are in need. Churches that fit this description become unhealthy because of unmet needs. Infighting is the result and division occurs.

Church health is maintained by a balanced approach to ministry. Proper emphasis must be placed on the areas of evangelism, discipleship, and ministry. A healthy church must be composed of members who share their personal story about Jesus out of a spirit-filled heart. This is our act of evangelism. A healthy church must assist new believers in their spiritual growth by encouraging them to live in purity and by leading them to discover their spiritual gifts. This is our act of discipleship. Finally, a healthy church must encourage maturing believers to participate in acts of service and function as part of the body of Christ. This is our act of ministry.

A Look at All Participants in the Church

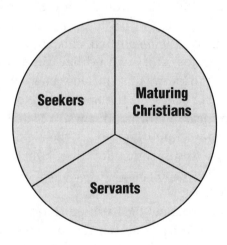

A balanced approach to ministry produces balanced results. Think of a pie divided into thirds. One third of those who participate in church ministries is lost and is seeking answers for life. Another third consists of newer believers who are maturing in their faith and discovering their spiritual gifts. The final third is defined as mature believers who are using their gifts in acts of servanthood. If we are expending a balanced effort that is empowered by God's Spirit in the areas of evangelism, discipleship, and ministry, this should be reflected in the outcome of these ministries.

Although our efforts play a significant role, the dynamics of a community and the congregation may cause the results to vary. For example, in some rural areas, the population of a community may consist of mostly Christian residents. This will reduce the number of unsaved individuals who participate in the ministries of the church. Also, a church may be a new congregation in a metropolitan area. In this case, there may be a much larger percentage of unbelievers participating in ministries within the church. We must consider factors such as these if we are to properly understand how well the church is succeeding.

Beginning with the End Result in Mind

We are to begin with the end in mind. This great leadership principle is very relevant. The end result God desires is that the body of Christ function as servants. We are saved for this purpose, and the success of this endeavor begins with those who lead. Leaders must be appropriate models for the congregation by being the servants that God requires. Paul wrote:

> It was he who gave some to be apostles, some to be prophets, some to be evangelists, and some to be pastors and teachers, to prepare God's people for works of service, so that the body of Christ may be built up until we all reach unity in the faith and in the knowledge of the Son of God and become mature, attaining to the whole measure of the fullness of Christ."
>
> —Ephesians 4:11–13

The role of leaders is to prepare God's people for works of service. They are not to be hired hands that do the ministry of the church. They are to be equippers who train believers to serve so that the body of Christ may be built up. The body of Christ is to be built up in spiritual stamina, having members with pure hearts, prepared to practice the spiritual exercise of servanthood. The body of Christ is also to be built up in size, as new believers join the kingdom of God. They are beginning a journey that will result in service, a role already established for them by God.

How will God use you to improve the health of the church and build up the body of Christ?

2

THE PASSION

Jesus replied: "'Love the Lord your God with all your heart and with all your soul and with all your mind.' This is the first and greatest commandment. And the second is like it: 'Love your neighbor as yourself.' All the Law and the Prophets hang on these two commandments.

—MATTHEW 22:37–40

Leading and Living Out of a Heart for God

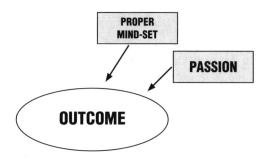

Karen Watson, a missionary to Iraq, was killed along with four other missionaries on March 15, 2004. Before she left, she wrote her pastors a letter that was to be opened only if she died on the mission field. The following is a portion of what she wrote:

> I thank you all so much for your prayers and support. Surely your reward in heaven will be great. Thank you for investing in my life and spiritual wellbeing. Keep sending missionaries out. Keep raising up fine young pastors. In regards to any service, keep it small and simple. Yes, simply, just preach the gospel...Be bold and preach the life-saving, life-changing, forever-eternal gospel. Give glory and honor to the Father. The Missionary heart: Care more than some think is wise; risk more than some think is safe; dream more than some think is practical; expect more than some think is possible. I was called not to comfort or success but to obedience...There is no joy outside of knowing Jesus and serving him.[1]

These words come from a passionate heart. Karen's last two statements are powerful. What would happen in our churches if we felt that we were called not to comfort or success but to obedience? I as a pastor feel convicted by her statements. We are all called to be missionaries to our mission fields. She was willing to lose her life for serving her God. I must be willing to make the necessary sacrifices to be obedient to my call to service in my mission field. This willingness to sacrifice comes from a passion for God.

What would happen in our communities if the members of our churches believed that there was no joy outside of knowing Jesus and serving Him? We experience joy when we live up to God's expectations for us to be His servants. The believer who accomplishes this realizes that there is no greater joy. As a leader, I must be willing to make the necessary sacrifices to influence the people in the church to experience this joy. If the church is not succeeding in this responsibility, changes must be made.

A Choice of the Heart

Our hearts will do one of two things: they will either unite us or divide us. Those who have the same passions are unified, while those who have conflicting passions are divided. The hearts of church members direct the journey of the local church. Members who operate as the true body of Christ have the heart of Christ. Jesus came for a reason—to seek and to save the lost (Luke 9:10). This was His passion.

The church, the body of Christ, should have the same desire. Jesus served others in an effort to reach them with the message of salvation. He ministered to win the right to be heard. He was willing to do whatever it took to accomplish this, whether it was touching a man considered unclean because of leprosy (Luke 5:12–14), taking time to speak with love to a woman who had been caught in adultery (John 8:3–11), inviting Himself to eat with a sinful tax collector (Luke 19:1–10), or giving His life on the cross (Matt. 27:35).

A passion for God results in unity. The psalmist wrote, "How good and pleasant it is when brothers live together in unity!" (Psalm 133:1). Jesus prayed that we would have unity. He said to the Father, "I have given them the glory that you gave me, that they may be one as we are one: I in them and you in me. May they be brought to complete unity to let the world know that you sent me and have loved them even as you have loved me" (John 17:22–23). Jesus desired that we would be unified in our effort to reveal the love of Christ to others. We too should desire this unity.

We should be passionate about becoming more united and less divided as God's people, as a nation, and as citizens of our world. The breakup of local churches is evidence that we as God's people are divided. The 2004 presidential election between George W. Bush and John Kerry revealed just how divided we are as a nation. The onslaught of terrorism around the world is a tragic testimony to the extreme differences that exist in the human family. Unity will come in only one way. We become unified when we agree to agree with God. I believe that we can become more united and less divided. How will this take place? One heart at a time! Paul wrote:

> Now to him who is able to establish you by my gospel and the proclamation of Jesus Christ, according to the revelation of the mystery hidden for long ages past, but now revealed and made known through the prophetic writings by the command of the eternal God, so that all nations might believe and obey him—to the only wise God be glory forever through Jesus Christ! Amen.
>
> —ROMANS 16:25–27

God has developed an organization to bring this change in our culture, and it is called the local church. We as Christ's body have tremendous power from God to bring change in our world. Unfortunately, many churches are doing more harm than good. They are not sacrificing and unleashing the tremendous power of God's love. Instead, they are separating themselves from society and attempting to protect themselves from evil in the world. The best protection from evil is to convert evil into good, and we are called to be part of this process.

INSTITUTION VS. MOVEMENT

Our passions motivate us and move us in certain directions. Church leaders who are effective have a willingness to do whatever it takes to reach the lost. This is their passion. Leaders in the church should desire that all people experience cleansing and release from the guilt that separates us from God. Our passion for God and those He has created will lead us away from the protective walls of our church buildings and take us into the world where people are in need. Leaders in a healthy church influence the body to become part of a movement to reach people in the world.

Erwin Raphael McManus, a church growth expert and pastor, wrote about the potential of the church in his book *An Unstoppable Force*:

The problem is that we treat the church as an organization instead of an organism. Even an elementary reading of the New Testament would make it clear that the church is the body of Christ. The church in her essence is a living system. Whenever we see the church through the template of an organization, we begin creating an institution. When we relate to the church as an organism, we begin to awaken an apostolic ethos, which unleashes the movement of God. The power and life of God's Spirit working in his people result in nothing less than cultural transformation.[2]

The healthy church is to be alive with God's love. The church truly is an organism that lives to help people discover God in a real and personal way.

Where will your heart take you? If you are a leader who is passionate about God, your love will lead you and those who follow you on a journey to become a healthy church, a fully functioning body of Christ. If you are a church member who is passionate about God, your heart will lead you to become involved in a ministry movement, using your spiritual gifts in acts of service and mission.

MANMADE TRADITIONS OR GOD'S COMMANDS?

In his book *Classic Christianity* Bob George wrote this great statement: "If truth is what sets us free, then error is what binds us."[3] Many in the church are bound by false beliefs created in the mind of man and are passionate about pressuring others to conform to man-made ideals. This error binds people, and they are unable to experience the joy that comes when we conform to the image of Christ and His servanthood. Those who conform to the image of Christ bring glory to God, while those who conform to the expectations of man bring glory only to man.

Jesus confronted those who lived according to man-made expectations and had elevated views of their own spiritual condition. He responded to religious leaders who measured spirituality on the basis of eating food with unclean hands and said:

"Isaiah was right when he prophesied about you hypocrites; as it is written:

> 'These people honor me with their lips, but their hearts are far from me. They worship me in vain; their teachings are but rules taught by men.' You have let go of the commands of God and are holding on to the traditions of men.'" And he said to them: "You have a fine way of setting aside the commands of God in order to observe your own traditions! For Moses said, 'Honor your father and your mother,' and, 'Anyone who curses his father or mother must be put to death.' But you say that if a man says to his father or mother: 'Whatever help you might otherwise have received from me is Corban' (that is, a gift devoted to God), then you no longer let him do anything for his father or mother. Thus you nullify the word of God by your tradition that you have handed down. And you do many things like that."
>
> —MARK 7:6–13

Jesus was very pointed in this statement to the Pharisees. He said that "these people honor me with their lips, but their hearts are far from me." They had developed their own path to God, a path that was dependent upon their own ability, not the love of God. They believed that their worth was determined by their success in obeying man-made rules. They were living by a worldly theology based on works and, because of this, had self-righteous hearts.

These religious leaders were living in what Larry Crabb called the "Old Way."[4] This was prevalent in the Old Testament, when people worked for God or prayed to Him from a motivation not to serve but to receive a blessing. They actually developed this theology from Scripture. For example, the Bible says, "Carefully follow the terms of this covenant, so that you may prosper in everything you do" (Deuteronomy 29:9). In this verse, it seems that God is setting us up to live for the blessing. However, the truth is that the covenant was a covenant of love and the people could not keep it unless they loved God more than all else. Their love for God would lead them to carefully follow the terms of the covenant, which would encourage God to bring prosperity into their life. Believers are to love God with a desire to bless Him. They are not to obey God in some sick effort to control the blessings they receive from Him.

It appears that many in Jesus' day were attempting to control God. Crabb called this way of life the "Law of Linearity."[5] To approach things in a linear fashion means that if we do "A," then "B" will happen. If we obey the commands, we will receive a blessing and prosper in everything we do.

Our passion should not be to receive blessing but to be a blessing. Those who live to receive blessing are self-centered and attentive to what others do for them. They see church only as a place where people should minister to their needs, and they care only about what they want. Those who live to be a blessing, however, are selfless. They are attentive to the needs of others and how God can use them in ministry. Wouldn't you love to be in a church filled with people who long to be a blessing rather than to be blessed?

We are a blessing to God when we fulfill our role of service. Unfortunately, many people measure others by the standard of man-made requirements. God requires that we love Him with all that we are—heart, mind, soul, and body. Jesus confronted the religious leaders about what they had been doing. He said, "They worship me in vain; their teachings are but rules taught by men. You have let go of the commands of God and are holding on to the traditions of men" (Mark 7:7–8). What a powerful statement! We have a choice to make. We can either hold on to the commands of God or we can hold on to the traditions of man. The decision has everything to do with our passions. If our passion is for God, we will do everything according to His commands. If our passion is for self, we will hold forth man-made expectations to show others how special we are.

God's command is clear. "The entire law is summed up in a single command: 'Love your neighbor as yourself'" (Gal. 5:14). In the Old Testament, God commanded His people to love the Lord their God with all their heart and with all their soul and with all their strength. This commandment was to be upon their hearts (Deut. 6:5–6). Jesus elaborated on this command when the religious leaders tried to trap Him. The Sadducees and the Pharisees had differing beliefs on which commands took precedence over others, and one of the Pharisees asked Jesus to identify the greatest commandment in the law:

> Jesus replies: "'Love the Lord your God with all your heart and with all your soul and with all your mind.' This is the first and greatest commandment. And the second is like it: "Love your neighbor as yourself." All the Law and the Prophets hang on these two commandments.
> —MATTHEW 22:37–40

Jesus' answer simplifies our lives. Everything we do should prove our love for God. Also, we prove our love for God by loving our neighbor. Jesus' final statement is critical to every decision we make. He said that all the laws God gave and all the instruction from God's prophets hang on these two commandments. In the same way, everything in our personal lives should reflect obedience to these two commandments.

We can also apply this to the life of the church. Every decision should be made for one reason and one reason only—to prove our love for God. The church proves its love for God when its members show love to those around them. We should evaluate every action in life by asking, "How does this action prove our love for God?" We should evaluate every activity, event, and program in the church by asking, "How does this ministry prove our love for God?" The church is not established to preserve the traditions of men, but to be the body of Christ and prove its love for God by serving others.

A Passion for God

Church leaders must determine if the church is operating out of a passion for God or a worldly passion that focuses on man's ability to follow traditions. A Godly passion directs us toward others and leads us to love our neighbor. A worldly passion directs us toward self and influences us to improve our position at the expense of others. Churches composed of the latter group of people are hypocritical in nature. Jesus had much to say about the hypocrites of His day, and He taught that they did not have a heart for God. From His words, we learn that a hypocrite is one who performs actions from a passion for self and proves it by his behavior.

Jesus taught that hypocrites do three things. First, hypocrites shut the door to the kingdom of God. Jesus made this very clear when He said, "Woe to you, teachers of the law and Pharisees, you hypocrites! You shut the kingdom of heaven in men's faces. You yourselves do not enter, nor will you let those enter who are trying to" (Matt. 23:13). These hypocritical religious leaders were teaching man-made expectations that excluded others from the kingdom of God. We also become hypocritical when we have expectations that a person must meet. Hypocrites measure people according to factors such as race, wealth, position in society, or the ability to follow man-made rules. However, God does not measure us in this manner. He looks at our hearts.

Second, hypocrites use God to promote themselves. Jesus warned against this when He said, "So when you give to the needy, do not announce it with trumpets, as the hypocrites do in the synagogues and on the streets, to be honored by men. I tell you the truth, they have received their reward in full" (Matt. 6:2). We become hypocritical in this way when we are more concerned that others see us than that others see God through us.

Third, hypocrites say one thing and do another. Jesus said, "You hypocrites! Isaiah was right when he prophesied about you: 'These people honor me with their lips, but their hearts are far from me'" (Matt. 15:7–8). These verses clearly state that the words of the religious leaders did not match their hearts. Churches throughout the world are filled with people like this. They say the right things about God and their passion to serve Him, but they do not back up their words with action. Our churches will not succeed until our words define our actions.

We must discern if our statements of love for God match our actions. Love becomes our foundation when we focus on Christ's sacrifice. Paul dealt with the importance of having the right foundation when he wrote:

> By the grace God has given me, I laid a foundation as an expert builder, and someone else is building on it. But each one should be careful how he builds. For no one can lay any foundation other than the one already laid, which is Jesus Christ. If any man builds on this foundation using gold, silver, costly stones, wood, hay or straw, his work will be shown for what it is, because the Day will bring it to light. It will be revealed with fire, and the fire will test the quality of each man's work.
>
> —1 Corinthians 3:10–13

Jesus laid a foundation of sacrifice, and the Christian life is about sacrifice. Unfortunately, some church members seem unwilling to make the necessary sacrifices to reach others for Christ. I fear that many of the works performed in the church are nothing but kindling that will be burned away. Members who refuse to make needed changes tend to begin with their man-made traditions. They shut the door to the kingdom of God in the faces of those who refuse to conform to these traditions. They refuse to change and cannot understand why their church is not more successful in reaching others. Their solution is to work harder at making their existing program work. Many times, this does little to change the results.

Some are passionate about their church program because of what it does for them, not because it ministers to others. It is comfortable for them, and they expect their neighbors to conform to the church's methodology. This comes from a selfish heart, and it is an unrealistic expectation. These church members forget that many of the current ministries were begun to meet the needs of people. Sadly, at some point in time, the ministry program became more important than the needs of others.

This misdirected passion for maintaining ministries come at the expense of those who need new ministry approaches that will reveal the love of God in a more culturally relevant way. Many churches are aware of the changing culture but make a conscious decision not to be relevant. They plan their programs for people inside the church, not those who are outside.

A church is effective if its passion is directed not toward a program, but toward God first and then the people we serve. This gives a great sense of clarity for the purpose of each ministry within the church. Believers must be willing to do whatever it takes to share the good news in understandable ways, even if this requires change. Paul expressed this attitude when he said, "To the weak I became weak, to win the weak. I have become all things to all men so that by all possible means I might save some. I do all this for the sake of the gospel, that I may share in its blessings" (1 Cor. 9:22–23). Church leaders should not change programs just for the sake of change. Strategies and programs that continue to meet the needs of people should remain. However, those that do not successfully show our love for God and others should be altered or discontinued.

Paradigm Shift

Rick Warren's book *The Purpose Driven Church* has influenced many local churches to make a paradigm shift. The premise of his book is that everything in the church should be organized around the purposes of the church. Years ago, the programs developed in the church were established to accomplish its purposes. However, a shift took place several decades ago, changing the focus from purposes to programs. Purposes were sacrificed for the sake of maintaining current ministries, and this created a problem.

God didn't establish church programs in the Bible, but He did reveal His purposes. Everything we do in the church should be done, not to maintain its current ministries, but to ensure that its purposes are accomplished. Fulfilling these purposes through our service should be the passion of every leader and member in the local church.

A WILLINGNESS TO CHANGE

To shift from a program-driven church to a purpose-driven church requires change, and this can be difficult. Our passion for God should be the basis for change. Once again, we do not change for the sake of change, but to reach people with the good news of Jesus. The church is constantly in a state of transition as it meets the needs of people from new and different cultures. A healthy church has leaders who keep the attention of the church on God first and others second. Leaders in the church must teach the members that love for God requires our ministry to a hurting world.

How do we keep our attention on God? Through prayer! We will not succeed as a church if we do not pray. We cannot know God's heart unless we connect with Him through prayer. The Bible says, "'For I know the plans I have for you,' declares the LORD, 'plans to prosper you and not to harm you, plans to give you hope and a future. Then you will call upon me and come and pray to me, and I will listen to you. You will seek me and find me when you seek me with all your heart'" (Jer. 29:11–13). What a great promise! We find God when we seek Him with all our heart. He must be our passion. When we are passionate about God, we pray. We seek Him through prayer. This scripture also tells us that God has a plan for us. How will we know His plan unless we pray?

Richard Foster, an authority in the area of spiritual disciplines, wrote:

Prayer catapults us onto the frontier of the spiritual life. Of all the Spiritual Disciplines prayer is the most central because it ushers us into perpetual communion with the Father.[9]

He also discussed the fact that we change because we pray:

Real prayer is life creating and life changing....Prayer is the central avenue God uses to change us. If we are unwilling to change, we will abandon prayer as a noticeable characteristic of our lives. The closer we come to the heartbeat of God the more we see our need and the more we desire to be conformed to Christ.[6]

This is great encouragement! Our prayer life softens our heart toward God and fosters a willingness to follow the plans He has for us.

The change process in the church begins when its leaders and members commit themselves to pray and seek God's will. We need to pray that God will change our pattern of living to conform to His pattern. Paul wrote, "Do not conform any longer to the pattern of this world, but be transformed by the renewing of your mind. Then you will be able to test and approve what God's will is—his good, pleasing and perfect will" (Rom. 12:2). We change our mind when our mind is focused on Him through prayer.

Members are more willing to make necessary changes when their hearts are directed toward God. They are also willing to change when they can see how proposed changes allow them to serve God by serving others. A leader who tries to make changes without nurturing the hearts of church members toward a passion for God is committing leadership suicide. This will cause division rather than unity within the church. George Barna, researcher and author of *Grow Your Church From the Inside In,* wrote:

A great ministry to the unchurched does not just happen. Such a ministry is not only the result of a clear, thoughtful and well-articulated philosophy but also a commitment to adequate preparation of the congregation. The pastors of these churches have worked long and hard to get people in the right frame of mind so that the ministry is not a bunch of programs, but a group of loving people who really care about the spiritual health of others.[7]

Jim Herrington, Mike Bonem, and James Furr addressed the topic of creating urgency for change in their book *Creating Congregational Change: A Practical Guide for the Transformational Journey*. They wrote, "Creating urgency...refers to the energy and motivation for change that is generated by contrasting between an accurate perception of reality and God's ideal."[8] They explained:

> ...change is driven when a significant gap exists between a vision of the future that people sincerely desire to achieve and a clear sense that they are not achieving that vision. As this recognition grows, so does their willingness to change their perspective and to try new approaches. This is the point at which they are experiencing creative tension.[9]

This understanding of creating change is also taught in secular society. John Kotter, a professor at Harvard, wrote: "Establishing a sense of urgency is crucial to gaining needed cooperation."[10]

Thus, we conclude that church members are more willing to change when they experience tension because they are not accomplishing an objective that their heart desires. They recognize that their current methods of ministry are keeping them from accomplishing their goals, and they believe that change will assist them in reaching their goals. M. Scott Boren, an authority in the area of church transformation, taught about the importance of these issues when he wrote:

> In order for a person to adopt a new idea, he must experience dissatisfaction with the status quo. He must

know of a better way. And he must see the first steps to take. These three things must add up to be greater than the anticipated loss or pain that will result from the change.[11]

Producing Effective Change

Ineffective organizations can change and become effective. Kotter defined a practical eight-stage process to facilitate change in an ineffective organization.[12] Notice that the first stage is to "establish a sense of urgency." This is followed by specific tasks that assist in making changes.

Kotter's Change Process

1. *Establishing a Sense of Urgency.* This includes: (a) examining the market and competitive realities, and (b) identifying and discussing crises, potential crises, or major opportunities.

2. *Creating the Guiding Coalition.* This includes: (a) putting together a group with enough power to lead the change and (b) getting the group to work together like a team.

3. *Developing a Vision and Strategy.* This includes: (a) creating a vision to help direct the change effort and (b) developing strategies for achieving that vision.

4. *Communicating the Change Vision.* This includes: (a) Using every vehicle possible to constantly communicate the new vision and strategies and (b) having the guiding coalition role model the behavior expected of employees.

5. *Empowering Broad-Based Action.* This includes: (a) getting rid of obstacles, (b) changing systems or structures that undermine the change vision, and (c) encouraging risk taking and nontraditional ideas, activities, and actions.

6. *Generating Short-Term Wins.* This includes: (a) planning for visible improvements in performance, or "wins," (b) creating those wins, and (c) visibly recognizing and rewarding people who made the wins possible.

7. *Consolidating Gains and Producing More Change.* This includes: (a) using increased credibility to change all systems, structures, and policies that don't fit together and don't fit the transformation vision, (b) hiring, promoting, and developing people who can implement that change vision, and (c) reinvigorating the process with new projects, themes, and change agents.

8. *Anchoring New Approaches in the Culture.* This includes: (a) creating better performance through customer- and productivity-oriented behavior, more and better leadership, and more effective management, (b) articulating the connections between new behaviors and organizational success, and (c) developing means to ensure leadership development and succession.

The remainder of this book will address many of these issues. We will learn how to develop a plan of ministry to reach our marketplace. Our goal is to help people experience the life-giving love of Christ and develop them into His servants.

3

THE PURPOSE

Many are the plans in a man's heart, but it is the
Lord's purpose that prevails.

—Proverbs 19:21

A Church Determined
to Satisfy God's Desires

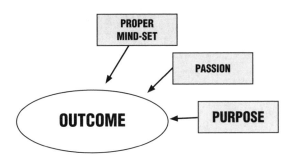

The launch of the space shuttle is one of the most amazing sights Florida residents have the opportunity to witness. About three or four years ago, I turned on the television and noticed on a news station that the shuttle was about to launch. I hurried outside my home in Bradenton (which is on the other side of the state from Cape Canaveral) to witness this incredible sight and stood in awe as I watched the flaming exhaust move slowly upward in the sky.

The space shuttle is able to complete its journey because of the collective effort of thousands of employees. They work together diligently on their mission to ensure that the space flight is a success. *Mission* is a word that is heard frequently around the space program. For example, there is "mission control," an area where key leaders gather to make certain that the mission is running smoothly. Their task is to accomplish the specific goals defined by NASA, and the mission is deemed successful if these goals are met.

The church is also a mission organization. I was taught this concept in seminary and have heard it throughout the years, but I did not really grasp the true importance of it until I read Rick Warren's book *The Purpose Driven Church*. Warren emphasized the importance of mission when he wrote: "The first task of leadership is to define the mission…"[1] Can you imagine what would happen in the space program if the mission were not defined? There would be many more tragic accidents than those we have regrettably witnessed. Unfortunately, tragedies take place in the church because the key leaders—the Mission Control Team—fail to define and properly carry out the mission.

Shortly after I read Warren's book, I was called to my first and only pastorate to date. Before I arrived on site, I sat down and defined what the mission of the church should be. I needed clear, measurable goals to determine if I was succeeding or failing in my call to lead the local church. I did not want the church to become ineffective or divided because of my failure to lead the church to discover its kingdom mission.

KEY TRUTHS ABOUT PURPOSE

The healthy church clearly understands its mission. We must consider key truths about our mission if we are to function properly. These truths define purpose and emphasize the importance of operating with purpose in the local church. Rick Warren and other experts have shown how establishing purpose produces positive effects on organizational life. Let's consider some of them.

1. Purpose determines our mission. We must have a clear understanding of what God wants us to accomplish. As we serve Him out of love, He must direct us in the process. His purposes become the framework for constructing a New Testament church.

   Warren described a process for accomplishing purpose when he wrote: "First, you must define your purposes. Next, you must communicate those purposes to everyone in your church—on a regular basis. Third, you must organize your church around your purposes. Finally, you must apply your purposes to every part of your church."[2] Following this process ensures that God's purpose for the church will become the foundation on which we build a program of ministries.

2. A clear purpose sets the agenda. Defining the agenda helps us make changes in the church when it is necessary. Alan Nelson and Gene Appel, experts in the area of transitioning, refer to a change sequence introduced by Everett M. Rogers in their book *How to Change Your Church Without Killing It*.[3] The sequence begins with setting the agenda and is followed by matching solutions to problems.

   Setting the agenda reveals problems that exist within an organization. Erwin Raphael McManus wrote: "After you expound the purpose, you then expose the problems."[4] Problems occur in areas where current methodology does not assist the church in fulfilling its purpose. The third part of Rogers's sequence is redefining and restructuring. The organization changes structures to make certain that the agenda is met. The organization begins to make changes to correct the problems that exist.

3. Purpose unifies us.[5] The Bible tells us that "where there is no vision, the people perish..." (Prov. 29:18, kjv). Warren wrote, "I believe it is also true that where there is no vision, people leave for another parish."[6] Maybe you can relate to this statement. Ministry partners in the church want to know why they are needed. They want to be an important part of the ministry team. Morale is built and momentum is created when there is a sense of purpose.

   McManus dealt with the importance of momentum and introduced a formula for it. He wrote:

   > The formula for momentum is $P=MV(2)$. "P" being momentum, "M" equaling mass, and "V" equaling velocity... Mass equals people. Without people there is no momentum. When people move together with common purpose, momentum happens.[7]

   He further explained:

   > Velocity is different. It always specifies a direction. So while speed is about motion, velocity is about movement. Velocity is speed with somewhere to go. Velocity is speed with a purpose, speed with intentionality. Velocity made human is action with direction. It is speed focused around a goal.[8]

   > "Speed," McManus concluded, "is determined by one's level of responsiveness to God's commands. Obedience is the spiritual equivalent of speed."[9]

Our ultimate purpose is to be obedient to God. The larger the group of obedient ministry partners, the greater the momentum as we move together, fulfilling God's purposes with one heart and mind.

4. Having a clear purpose reduces frustration.[10] Warren wrote, "The secret of effectiveness is to know what really counts, then do what really counts, and not worry about the rest."[11] Frustration diminishes in a culture of obedience to God's purposes. This redefines the church so that it is no longer a crowd of people with no direction, but a community of believers with great purpose. McManus wrote, "Uniting a crowd into a community requires spiritual leadership, and what emerges in the process is the generation of a common culture built upon commonly held beliefs, values, and worldviews."[12]

   Spiritual leadership is the key. Members of the Mission Control Team must clearly define the end result that God desires in the church, for this will keep the entire church unified. Frustration occurs when individuals are moving in multiple directions. Leaders have a tendency to blame the people in an organization for not being unified. However, many times the leader is to blame because he or she has not effectively defined the purpose.

5. Having a clear purpose encourages cooperation from others.[13] Warren wrote, "If you want your members to get excited about the church, actively support it, and generously give to it, you must vividly explain up front exactly where the church is headed."[14] Pat MacMillan, an expert in team leadership training, wrote: "A clear, common, compelling task that is important to the individual team members is the single biggest factor in team success. All the team workshops in the world pale to insignificance in comparison to a clear and challenging task or goal."[15]

A task or goal gives us something to align people in an organization. I think of automobiles when I think of the word alignment. Wheels that are not aligned cause a car to veer off course, and the driver must exert much energy to keep the car on the road. The solution to this problem is to have an expert perform an alignment on the car.

Church leaders must think of themselves as experts who perform an "alignment" of the church ministries. This occurs when there is a "link between the individual team member's goals and the team purpose."[16] Therefore the leader who performs an alignment must link the goals of members with the defined purpose. The absence of this link causes "misalignment," which pulls people away from the identified purpose.

Defining the purpose is not the only element that secures organizational success. Members of the team must have a desire for the purpose to be realized. Desire is the fuel that gives the team power. MacMillan taught:

When a team is in alignment, every member is highly committed to the team purpose. They are in the same boat, heading in the same direction, pulling together. Alignment provides the focus that unleashes the potential power of the team...When team members are in alignment, they are unified in their intentions. And because they are pulling together in the same direction, there is less wasted energy.[17]

Alignment causes an organization to experience what M. Scott Boren calls "critical mass." This occurs when "enough people are convinced, understand the technicalities of the vision, and are walking in unity."[18] Churches that do not experience "critical mass" become a "critical mess." The church that is a "critical mess" is composed of members who have desires for competing purposes. This causes division, and division causes the church to veer off course.

6. Having a purpose provides a means of measuring success.[19] We have learned that we should measure the success of a church by the number of people who are serving in the church. Having a purpose defines what we are to do in service to God and becomes a way to measure our success as servants of God. Warren taught, "How does church evaluate itself? Not by comparing itself to other churches, but by asking, 'Are we doing what God intends for us to do?'"[20]

What does God intend for you to do as a church? This is your purpose. Leaders must answer the question, "Are we fulfilling God's purposes for the church?" If the answer is yes, the body of Christ is healthy as it serves God by showing His love with one heart and mind. If the answer is no, attention must be given to the areas of misalignment.

The Purposes of the Church

Do you know what God intends for your church to do? Leaders must have a passion to discover and fulfill God's intention. This passion will cause the leader to open his or her eyes and search the Scriptures for God's plan. We can discover the purposes of the church simply by reading about the activities of the early church in the New Testament. Read the following passage and circle the action words.

> Peter replied, "Repent and be baptized, every one of you, in the name of Jesus Christ for the forgiveness of your sins. And you will receive the gift of the Holy Spirit. The promise is for you and your children and for all who are far off—for all whom the Lord our God will call." With many other words he warned them; and he pleaded with them, "Save yourselves from this corrupt generation." Those who accepted his message were baptized, and about three thousand were added to their number that day. They devoted themselves to the apostles' teaching and to the fellowship, to the breaking of bread and to prayer. Everyone was filled with awe, and many wonders

and miraculous signs were done by the apostles. All the believers were together and had everything in common. Selling their possessions and goods, they gave to anyone as he had need. Every day they continued to meet together in the temple courts. They broke bread in their homes and ate together with glad and sincere hearts, praising God and enjoying the favor of all the people. And the Lord added to their number daily those who were being saved.

—ACTS 2:38–47

The New Testament church was a church of action. Notice what they did.

- They devoted themselves to the apostles teaching. This was an act of discipleship.

- They met together and ate together. These were acts of fellowship.

- They sold their possessions and gave to those who were in need. These were acts of ministry.

- They praised God. This was an act of worship.

- God added to their number daily those who were being saved. This occurred because of acts of evangelism.

These five actions are the purposes of the church. Gene Mims defined these purposes in his book *The Kingdom Focused Church*:

> **Evangelism**—"The process of sharing the gospel with the lost and winning them to Christ, thereby enabling them to enter the kingdom of God."[21]

> **Discipleship**—"The process of teaching the new citizens in the kingdom of God to love, trust, and obey

Him, and teach them how to win and train others to do the same."[22]

Fellowship—"It is the result of the intimate spiritual relationship that Christians share with God and other believers through their relationship with Jesus Christ."[23]

Ministry—"…is meeting another person's needs in the name of Jesus, expressed as service to people inside the church family and expressed as missions to those outside the church with the resources God provides."[24]

Worship—"…is an activity in which believers experience God in a meaningful, spiritually transforming way."[25]

The healthy church aligns itself with each of these five purposes. They become our mission, the goals of the church, and are accomplished when the church acts as the body of Christ. Leaders, who serve as the Mission Control Team, must make certain that every ministry in the church is launched to accomplish one or more of these purposes. Leaders must also encourage members to become ministry partners and serve in these ministries.

A STATEMENT OF PURPOSE

It is vitally important that the Mission Control Team create a mission statement that clearly presents these purposes in a compelling manner. As I prepared for my first pastorate, I had the opportunity to dream about how our church could accomplish these ministry goals. I took pen and paper and wrote down ideas and words that were associated with both the purposes established by God and the unique characteristics of our church. From this beginning, our statement of purpose has evolved to say the following: "To show the love of Christ as we win the lost, build the saved, and care for the hurting, by becoming all things to all people."

Our purpose statement directs the attention of our ministry partners to each of the five purposes. We call our members "ministry partners," a name that communicates to our members that all of us are to be in ministry together. Accomplishing the purposes of the church requires us to partner together. Our purpose statement begins with love, which points to the purposes of worship and fellowship. We teach our ministry partners that love moves us toward the object of our worship. All of us worship someone or something because of our love, and the one we love the most is our object of worship. Our goal is to love God and to honor Him with our lives, and we will worship God when we love Him more than all else. Surrendering completely to God is our act of worship.

We also use the word *love* to draw attention to our involvement in fellowship. Love causes us to form relationships with others. Those who love to sail, have a tendency to hang out with people who like sailing. Those who love to golf like to hang out with golfers. Those who love Jesus want to hang out with people who love Jesus. This is our act of fellowship.

In addition, we teach that our love for Christ, revealed through our worship and fellowship, becomes the fuel for other activities. We talk about that which we love. Our love for Christ causes us to share the good news of His love with others, and this is our act of evangelism. We learn about that which we love. Our love for Christ influences us to learn more about Him, and this is our act of discipleship. We care for those we love. Our love for Christ causes us to help others through acts of service and mission. Our service is directed toward those in our church, and our mission is directed to those outside the church. This is our act of ministry.

Our purpose statement also includes a strategy for ministry. Paul wrote to the church in Corinth and said, "To the weak I became weak, to win the weak. I have become all things to all men so that by all possible means I might save some" (1 Cor. 9:22). Paul reached out to others by becoming all things to all people.

We have adopted this as a strategy for accomplishing God's purposes within the church. We become softball players to reach softball players. We become boaters to reach boaters. We become racquetball players to reach racquetball players. This applies not only to areas of interest, but also to other areas. The more diverse our congregation becomes in ethnic background, predominant language, religious background, and interests, the more our mission field expands. All ministry partners bring a unique circle of influence with them. They have relationships, cultural backgrounds, and interests that allow them to have influential ministries as a part of the body of Christ.

An effective purpose statement meets some specific criteria. It must be clear, compelling, and measurable, and it should answer three important questions. 1) Do I understand the purpose and goals? 2) Are the goals worth my sacrifice? 3) Am I willing to be held accountable for reaching these goals? The Mission Control Team must create a purpose statement that encourages people to say yes to all three questions. God's purposes are powerful enough for all of us and should be communicated with conviction, passion, and enthusiasm.

EACH PROBLEM REQUIRES THE ATTENTION OF MISSION CONTROL LEADERS

The Mission Control Team is responsible for diagnosing problems and working to make corrections when believers are unwilling to fulfill the established purposes. It must understand what causes this. The problem may be a lack of leadership commitment to accomplish the purpose, poor communication about the purpose, or believers who have a wrong passion and are unwilling to follow God's will concerning ministry.

As we mentioned before, every effort must be made to ensure that all leaders are aligned with the purposes. There must be a "whatever it takes" mentality among those in leadership positions, and this occurs when they are committed to God. Leaders must hold one another accountable for their practice of faith disciplines. Personal time with God is critical to the development of a committed heart, and this begins with our prayer life.

Leaders must make certain that the purposes are before the people in clear and creative ways. This will keep the focus where it should be. Believers will drift off course if the destination determined by the purposes is not regularly before them. NASA's Mission Control team would be quite upset if a mission to Mars failed because an astronaut became infatuated with the moon and changed his course.

Finally, leaders must speak the truth of God's Word about His desires. We are able to accomplish God's purposes when our hearts are committed to follow Him. Remember, a healthy church is composed of members who have a passion for God. We do what we do to show our love for God, and we show our love for God by serving others. He must be our hearts desire, our object of worship. The Mission Control Leadership Team must continue to create tension by helping people discover those with unmet needs.

This chapter has shown the importance of having a purpose and a Mission Control Team that works toward its completion. Are you committed to be a part of the Mission Control Team? You can better answer this question by answering two additional questions. Are you aligned with the purposes of the church? Do you have a passion to fulfill God's purposes for the church? This passion confirms your calling and will cause you to have a "whatever it takes" attitude. I encourage you to do whatever it takes to become the leader or member that God can use.

4

THE PLAN

But the plans of the LORD stand firm forever, the
purposes of his heart through all generations.
—PSALM 33:11

A Blueprint for Work in the Church

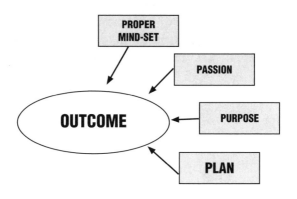

C hoosing a design plan for a new house can be a challenging experience. My family has gone through this process on two occasions, and I have learned that husbands and wives can have very different tastes. One of the greatest developments in the housing market is the model home. Some like to visit model homes just for fun. How do I know this? You guessed it! My wife and I have had wonderful dates just checking out the latest "cribs" (If you don't know what a "crib" is, it may be time to get "hip" with the latest youth culture). We dreamed about having certain products or features that were in those homes. This can be both fun and frustrating, depending on the size of the checking account.

These visits took on much greater significance when we were actually preparing to buy a new house for our family. Our goal, after finally deciding on a house plan, was for the completed house to look like the designers plans. Fortunately, this has been a great experience for us. However, I can't say that for everyone. Workers who don't pay attention to the details can produce homes that are far less than that which is desired.

Contractors should not build without a design plan. Neither should church leaders attempt to construct the local church without a design plan for ministry. The goal of this chapter is to provide a design plan by which we can fulfill the purposes of the church as a local body of believers.

A Plan for Moving People Closer to God

God has a plan for all of us. Paul explained this when he wrote, "For we are God's workmanship, created in Christ Jesus to do good works, which God prepared in advance for us to do" (Eph. 2:10). God desires that we become His servants, and we have no business altering His final design plan. The church is established to help this design plan become a reality by producing servants who fulfill the purposes of God. The health of the church is dependent upon the creation of a ministry plan that accomplishes God's purposes for the church. As we learned in chapter three, the Mission

Control Team has the responsibility to produce a plan that will accomplish this end result.

According to *Webster's New World Dictionary*, a plan is "a scheme for making, doing, or arranging something…"[1] The goal of the church is to develop servants of God who are fully devoted to Him. Fully devoted followers fulfill the purposes of worship, fellowship, evangelism, discipleship, and ministry, as we learned in the previous chapter. William Bridges wrote about the four "P's" that are necessary for successful organizations in his book *Managing Transitions: Making the Most of Change.* He said that a transitioning organization, which accurately defines a church, must 1) have a clear purpose, 2) have a clear picture of what it is to do, 3) have a plan, and 4) give people a part to play.[2] We will learn a strategy that meets these four criteria.

The design plan we provide in this chapter is a spiritual construction plan that will help us produce servants who are functioning parts of the body of Christ. We will accomplish this by first defining some important terms that identify various groups of people found in our world. Generally, in a spiritual context, all of humanity can be described by one of the following words.

1. The Seeker = someone who does not know God and is searching for answers in life. People in this group are lost and are looking for true happiness. They have not yet accepted the forgiveness God offers them through Jesus' death and resurrection. We know that Jesus came to reach this group of people. He said, "For the Son of Man came to seek and to save what was lost" (Luke 19:10).

2. The Saved = someone who has received forgiveness for his sins and has given Jesus control of his life. People in this group have begun their Christian journey. Those who come to Christ receive God's great promise, "for, 'Everyone who calls on the name of the Lord will be saved'" (Rom. 10:13).

3. The Servant = someone who has matured in his Christian faith to the point that he has discovered his spiritual gifts and has begun using his gifts in acts of ministry. Jesus said, "Now get up and stand on your feet. I have appeared to you to appoint you as a servant and as a witness of what you have seen of me and what I will show you" (Acts 26:16). Servants use their spiritual gifts to reveal God's love.

Church leaders have two responsibilities in relating to these groups of people. They are responsible to lead the seeker to be saved and to lead the saved to become servants. Remember, servants are the end result that God desires. This process is illustrated below:

From Seeker to Servant

Seeker   Saved   Servant

A STRATEGY ORGANIZED WITH PURPOSE

Church activity that leads a seeker to be saved is called evangelism. Church activity that leads one who is saved to become a servant is called discipleship. And church activity that leads a servant into action is called ministry. This is illustrated in the diagram below:

Identification of Ministry Performance

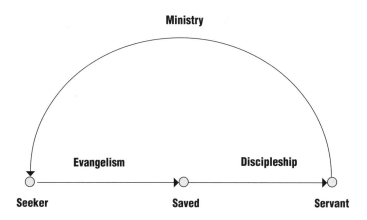

You will notice in the diagram above that three of the five purposes—evangelism, discipleship, and ministry—are represented. But where do fellowship and worship fit in? We have previously learned that our love is directed toward those we worship and that we form relationships with others and fellowship with them because of the object of our love. The love we have for Christ is at the heart of our plan for ministry. Our love for Him leads us to worship Him and to develop relationships with others who also love Him. This is illustrated in the following diagram:

The Plan Focused on God's Purposes

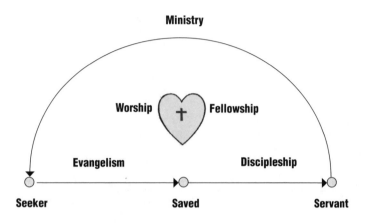

The arrows represent movement in specific directions. For example, the servant directs ministry to the seeker. All servants have the responsibility to share Christ with a lost world. Jesus gave us a commission: "Go into all the world and preach the good news to all creation" (Mark 16:15). This is the beginning point of ministry for all servants, but it is not their only ministry. Ministry can also be directed toward people who find themselves in the process of moving from being saved to becoming a servant. All of us are located somewhere along the connecting arrows between the words *seeker* and *saved* and the words *saved* and *servant*. A servant aims his ministry toward people at these location points. This is illustrated below:

The Servant's Aim of Ministry

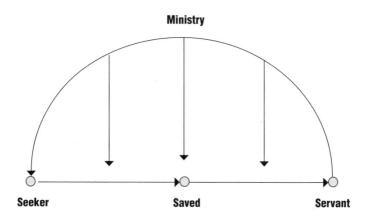

COMPLETING THE STRATEGY MAP

We can better identify the location points of people who are in the process of becoming servants by using identification points. They are represented by larger arrows that specify various groups of people.

The Completed Strategy Map

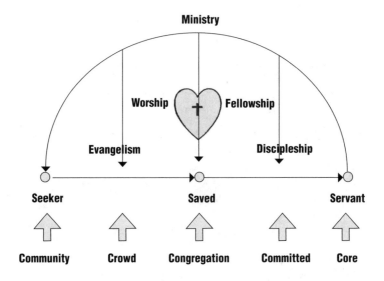

The groups identified in the illustration were described by Rick Warren.[3] He illustrated these groups by using five concentric circles, with the outer circle representing the "Community" and the inner circle representing the "Core." The groups are illustrated in the above design in a linear fashion, showing a distinct movement from one location to the other. This allows us to have a working strategy map to plan actions of ministry to reach each people group. The five groups are defined as follows:

1. Community = Unchurched. This group includes unsaved individuals living in the ministry area of the church.

2. Crowd = Attenders. This group consists of the unsaved that have made a connection to the local church.

3. Congregation = Members. This group includes Christians who are not members of the local church and Christians who are members of the local church.

4. Committed = Maturing Members. This group includes individuals who have begun maturing in their faith by practicing the disciplines of the faith as members of the local church.

5. Core = Lay Ministers. This group includes individuals who have discovered their spiritual gifts and have begun using them in acts of service.

LOCATING GROUP STRUCTURES ON THE STRATEGY MAP

How do we minister to each of these groups? Although we do not see the establishment of specific programs in the Bible, we do see the presence of group structures. Gene Mims, in his book *The Kingdom Focused Church*, focused attention on four specific group structures that can be seen in the ministry of Jesus. These four groups were not only important in Jesus' ministry, but they are also important in the ministry of the church. Each group helps the church accomplish its purposes.

The Bible says:

> Jesus went through all the towns and villages, teaching in their synagogues, preaching the good news of the kingdom and healing every disease and sickness. When he saw the crowds, he had compassion on them, because they were harassed and helpless, like sheep without a shepherd. Then he said to his disciples, "The harvest is plentiful but the workers are few. Ask the Lord of the harvest, therefore, to send out workers into his harvest field."
>
> —MATTHEW 9:35–38

The following group structures are present in this passage. They are defined by Gene Mims as follows:

1. Corporate Worship—"...exists for believers to celebrate God's grace and mercy, to proclaim God's truth, and evangelize the lost in an atmosphere of encountering the presence, holiness, and revelation of Almighty God."[4] Jesus taught in their synagogues and preached the good news. The synagogue was their place of corporate worship.

2. Open Groups—"...exist to lead people to faith in Christ and to build believers by engaging them in evangelism, discipleship, fellowship, ministry, and worship."[5] Jesus had compassion on the crowds as He saw them harassed and helpless, like sheep without a shepherd. The crowds represent people groups who are lost and need to be reached.

3. Closed Groups—"...exist to build kingdom leaders and to equip believers to serve the Lord."[6] Jesus taught His disciples about the harvest and said the workers were few. This was directed to a closed group, those who were committed to Him.

4. Ministry Teams—"...exist to build up the body of Christ to accomplish the work of service within the church and to advance the kingdom of God throughout the world. The work of kingdom advance is a work of beginning new kingdom communities with an urgency to reach those without Christ."[7] Jesus directed the disciples to ask the Lord of the harvest to send workers into His harvest field. The workers represent ministry teams who perform acts of ministry to those in need.

These four groups can be used to reach the different people groups represented on the Strategy Map. This is illustrated in the following diagram:

Mapping Group Structures on the Strategy Map

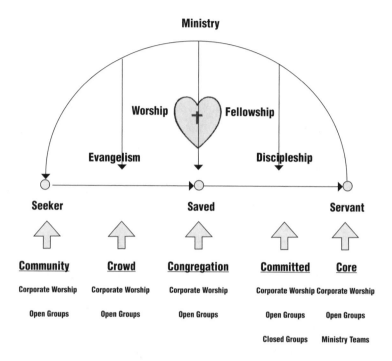

Notice that "Corporate Worship" is found under all the people groups. Worship should be conducted in a way that is understandable and relevant to those in the community (Community). It may be the first connection that people make to the church (Crowd). Christians, both members and non-members, participate in worship (Congregation). Members who are committed to grow deeper in their faith share in worship (Committed). Finally, members who use their gifts in acts of ministry are involved in the worship experience (Core).

Open groups are also found under each of the people group headings. These are small groups that operate like small churches and fulfill the same purposes performed by the church as a whole. An open group is a place for people to find community by connecting with the crowd, discovering Christ and becoming a part of the congregation, becoming committed as they mature in their faith, and becoming involved in ministry as they use their spiritual gifts for God's glory. It is known as a cell group, or a Sunday school group that functions as a cell group.

True Sunday school groups are open groups. Sunday school has been defined by Ken Hemphill and Bill Taylor, experts in the field of small groups. They wrote, "the foundational strategy in a local church for leading people to faith in the Lord Jesus Christ and for building on-mission Christians through open Bible study groups that engage people in evangelism, discipleship, ministry, fellowship, and worship."[8]

Cell groups in our church are called L.I.F.E. Groups. They focus on ministry through the letter "L" (loving those both inside and outside the group); evangelism through the letter "I" (inviting the lost and unchurched to attend the group); worship and fellowship through the letter "F" (fellowshipping with God and others); and discipleship through the letter "E" (equipping others with the truth of God's Word for personal growth and acts of service). Guests can enter an open group at any time. This is why they are called "open groups."

"Closed groups" are located under the "committed" people group. These are training groups for believers only and are dedicated to Christian growth or preparation for ministry tasks. Involvement in these groups requires a certain level of commitment.

Finally, you will notice that "Ministry Teams" are located under the "Core" people group. We consider anyone who has a ministry to be part of the core of the church. They serve on ministry teams that are aimed toward the community, crowd, congregation, or committed people groups. Ministry Team members serve out of their personal relationship with God. This does not mean that others, even lost people, may not work in the church. However, they do their work, not because they are servants of God who long to honor Him, but because they are seeking fulfillment through their own self effort.

Ministry teams are groups of people who work together to accomplish critical tasks in the church. Open groups, corporate worship, and closed groups all require ministry teams to function properly. Other ministry activities in the church also require ministry team volunteers. These are described below.

ADDITIONAL MINISTRY ACTIVITIES

The four group structures previously mentioned are emphasized in God's Word. I would like to add some other ministry functions to the map. These new ministry functions are highlighted in the diagram entitled "Additional Ministry Functions."

1. **Personal Evangelism.** This appears under the "Community" people group. Personal evangelism is the act in which a believer shares the good news of Jesus Christ with a non-believer in his circle of influence. He does this by telling the story of his personal encounter with Christ and inviting others to make the same commitment. He may also lead individuals toward Christ by inviting them to programs and events that encourage seekers to be saved.

   According to George Barna, 73 percent of the unchurched have never been invited to church.[9] The field is ripe for harvest, and we must work the fields. Jesus told His disciples, "The harvest is plentiful but the workers are few. Ask the Lord of the harvest, therefore, to send out workers into his harvest field" (Matt. 9:37–38).

   Again and again we see that Jesus had encounters with people—the religious, the sick, the thieves, the adulterers, the prostitutes, and the demon possessed. Jesus had a story to tell them, a message of good news. We as believers also have a story to tell, and it too is a story of good news. We are living examples of what God can do with sinful humanity. He gives us abundant life. Jesus said, "The thief comes only to steal and kill and destroy;

Additional Ministry Functions

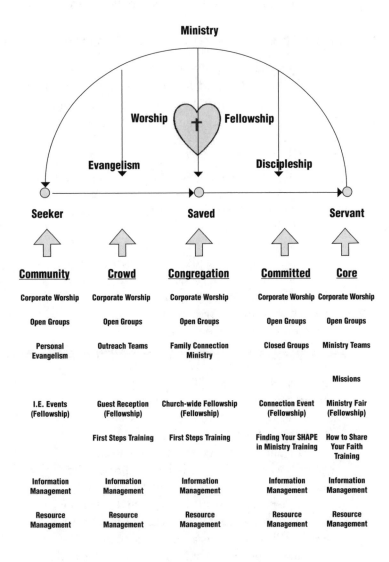

Community	Crowd	Congregation	Committed	Core
Corporate Worship	Corporate Worship	Corporate Worship	Corporate Worship	Corporate Worship
Open Groups	Open Groups	Open Groups	Open Groups	Open Groups
Personal Evangelism	Outreach Teams	Family Connection Ministry	Closed Groups	Ministry Teams
				Missions
I.E. Events (Fellowship)	Guest Reception (Fellowship)	Church-wide Fellowship (Fellowship)	Connection Event (Fellowship)	Ministry Fair (Fellowship)
	First Steps Training	First Steps Training	Finding Your SHAPE in Ministry Training	How to Share Your Faith Training
Information Management	Information Management	Information Management	Information Management	Information Management
Resource Management	Resource Management	Resource Management	Resource Management	Resource Management

I have come that they may have life, and have it to the full" (John 10:10). The success of the evangelistic efforts of the church is dependent upon the people who compose the body of Christ. They must share the message of hope with those who are seeking answers in life.

2. **Outreach Teams.** This ministry appears under the "Crowd" people group. People who are part of the "Crowd" have made a connection to the church through the personal invitation of members. Outreach teams are groups of people who intentionally make further contact with these people.

   Our outreach teams are organized through our segment ministries and open small groups. Segment ministries are aimed at different segments of our population, including our children's, youth, singles, young married, middle-aged married, and senior adult ministries. Outreach teams represent each segment ministry. The outreach teams for our open small groups make contact with those who have attended the open small group meetings or events sponsored by the group.

   The church as a whole, each segment ministry, and our open small groups continually generate new friendships with people in the community. I prefer to think of new people who have connected with our church as "friends" and not "prospects." The word *prospect* takes something away from the personal nature of new relationships.

   Outreach team members deliver information to the homes of people in the community, highlighting the church worship services and other ministry segments that may be of interest. For example, our "new friend" may have children and want to know more about the children's ministry. Outreach teams also provide information in the form of a brochure about the church's beliefs on how to have a relationship with God.

The purpose for the contact is to continue to build the relationship, to share Christ if the opportunity arises, and to answer any questions about the church's ministry or beliefs. Outreach Teams also invite "new friends" to the L.I.F.E. Group and to the First Steps Training Class, which is held monthly and provides an overview of our beliefs, our purpose, and our organization.

3. **Family Connection Ministry.** This appears under the "Congregation" people group. This ministry connects new members to the church and meets their needs. Deacons fulfilled this ministry in the early church in the New Testament and had the responsibility to meet the material needs of people in the congregation. The Bible says:

   So the Twelve gathered all the disciples together and said,

   > It would not be right for us to neglect the ministry of the word of God in order to wait on tables. Brothers, choose seven men from among you who are known to be full of the Spirit and wisdom. We will turn this responsibility over to them and will give our attention to prayer and the ministry of the word.
   >
   > —ACTS 6:2–4

   The Deacon Ministry is vital in the life of the church. A healthy church has a system of ministry prepared to meet the needs of its people.

4. **Missions.** This ministry function appears under the "Core" people group. God has given each of us a mission to perform. The church is called to reach its mission field for Christ, and this requires the involvement of people who compose the "Core." Our mission is directed toward four areas—to people in

our immediate community, our state, our nation, and our world.

Specific ministry is aimed at each group. For example, our church has adopted local missions projects that feed the homeless and care for those who are pregnant; state missions programs that house children who have been separated from their families; a ministry to the homeless in Chicago, and a ministry in Honduras. These are some of our missions ministries.

5. **Fellowship Activities.** These activities are conducted to provide ministry to each people group. You will notice that there are fellowship activities directed toward each people group on the map. They include:

   A. Intentionally Evangelistic Events (I. E. E.). This ministry function appears under the "Community" people group. These events of interest are conducted to reach people in the "Community" and connect believers with unbelievers. The purpose is to share the message of God's love. Jesus had mass appeal. He conducted an intentionally evangelistic event when He used a boy's small portion of bread and fish to feed thousands. He used this event as a precursor to presenting the truth to those who needed salvation. (See John 6:5–29.)

   Intentionally Evangelistic Events are effective tools to use in sharing the good news with those in a community. People will come to a Spring Training Baseball Clinic, participate in a recreational league, attend a ladies luncheon on Mother's Day weekend, play in a golf tournament, go boating with their Christian friends, come to hear a professional athlete speak, or come to hear a former actress share her testimony. These are all examples of activities our church has conducted to connect with people who don't know Christ personally.

   We have found that many will not come to a worship service, but they will come to one of these

events. We have also found that people are more
likely to come to a worship experience after they
form relationships through these activities with multiple people in our church.

Another example of an I.E.E. is a new resident
connection day. The church could deliver welcome
gifts to new residents in their ministry area on this
day. This can be highly effective in communities
where there is rapid growth. Volunteers are not required to share the plan of salvation with these new
residents. The goal is to make people feel welcome
by helping them make an acquaintance in their new
community.

B. Guest Events. We hold these events to help
people who have connected with the church make
further friendships with staff and church members.
My wife and I host a monthly "Guest Reception" in
our home and invite all the "new friends" who have
been guests in our church. We do this on a Sunday
evening after our regular Sunday evening activities.
Our staff, along with some outreach team volunteers,
attends the event. We have found that a majority of
those who attend a guest reception either join our
fellowship or begin to regularly attend our church.

C. Churchwide Fellowship. These fellowships
provide an environment where church members
can get to know other members. Examples of these
events are Homecoming, Harvest Dinner at Thanks-
giving, Sunday Night Dessert Fellowships, and Dinner on the Grounds.

D. Connection Event. The purpose of this event
is to provide a non-threatening atmosphere where
members or guests who are not in a small group
can learn more about the groups that are available.
We host quarterly "Connection Events" and set
up display booths (tables) by the day of the week.
Each group has information available for prospective group members at the table that corresponds to
the day they meet. Leaders of these groups are also

available to answer questions. We serve Starbucks Cappuccino and donuts (or ice-cream for the Saturday night crowd).

E. Ministry Fair. This event provides information about ministry opportunities for those who are not involved in ministry. We conduct an annual "Ministry Fair" to promote both our ministries and also the Finding Your SHAPE in Ministry Class, which is offered monthly.

6. **First Steps Training.** This ministry appears under two people groups. The first is the "Crowd" people group. We invite all those who are interested in learning more about our church to attend our "First Steps Training Class." This gives us another connection point with new friends.

   "First Steps Training" is also found under the "Congregation" people group because the training is required for membership in our church. We want all our members to have an understanding of what it means to be part of the body of Christ. The class provides training on the beliefs of the church, the purposes of the church, the organization of the church, and how they can be involved on the church team. Paul wrote, "For physical training is of some value, but godliness has value for all things, holding promise for both the present life and the life to come" (1 Tim. 4:8). A healthy church has leaders who teach the basics of what it means to be involved in a church.

7. **Finding Your SHAPE in Ministry Training.** You will notice this training is included on the map under the "Committed" location point. Those who are growing in their faith should discover their spiritual gifts and learn the importance of using those gifts in acts of ministry. This typically takes place before they become involved in ministry.

8. **How to Share Your Faith Training.** The title of this training defines its focus. We teach individuals how to share Christ with those in their circles of influence. You will notice that this training is included under the "Core" location point on the map. Those who serve should be equipped to share their faith. They are winning the right to be heard through their acts of service, and they should know what to say to a person who becomes open to the message of Christ.

9. **Information Management.** You will find this ministry functions under all the people groups on the map. It is the management of information about people in our community and those who have made a connection with the church.

   The healthy church keeps accurate information on those who have been reached through the ministry of the church and uses this information to make outreach assignments and map individuals as they become involved in various ministries in the church. This is necessary in the process of leading people to become servants of God. If you do not keep accurate information, you will have no way to hold others accountable, and people will begin slipping through the cracks of ministry. You will learn later how to use information to map people in the church by using a Strategy People Map.

10. **Resource Management.** You will notice that "Resource Management" is also directed toward all the people groups on the map. This includes the management of finances, facilities, literature, transportation, and other resources that are critical to conducting ministry within the church. Ministry can happen only if the necessary resources are provided.

The group and ministry functions mentioned above are critical in a well balanced, healthy approach to our ministry of moving people from where they are to where God wants them to be—His servants. The Mission Control team is able to look at the group structures and ministry functions and make adjustments when success is not being realized. Are you willing to serve on a Mission Control Team?

5
THE POSITION

Teach me to do your will, for you are my God;
may your good Spirit lead me on level ground.
—PSALM 143:10

Determining the Spiritual Condition
of Those Affiliated With the Church

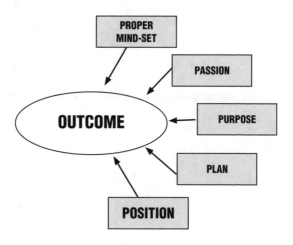

The evening has come and you have gathered with a new friend from work and some people from his church. You're new in town and you are excited to meet other residents in the community. Your company has transferred you here, and you want to make quick connections with those who live in the area.

Until now, your life has been measured by one goal—your position in the workplace. You've never really been around "religious" people very much, except for a short time during your childhood when your parents went through a momentary fixation on God. You are intrigued by what is to occur tonight because you've noticed something different about your friend. He seems to live his life with so much joy, something you really desire. The workplace isn't satisfying you the way you thought it would. Your professional goals are quickly being realized, but you still feel a sense of emptiness.

The event you are attending is a game night hosted by your friend's church, and you have gathered at a home to eat and to play a game called "Final Destination." The object of the game is to follow clues that lead you to each of five locations. Clues are given at each site and direct you on your journey. The team that arrives at the "final destination" first wins the game and is awarded a $50 gift certificate to a nice restaurant.

The teams approach the game with great enthusiasm. Each group receives their first clue and quickly jumps into their car to travel toward the first location. All the teams arrive within a three-minute time period of one another and begin reading the second clue. This clue is more difficult, and three of the five teams in the game arrive within five minutes of each other at the second location. Another team arrives about fifteen minutes later and the final group never shows up. They give up after they pass an area ice-cream store that is screaming out their names. The evening progresses, and at the end of the game, only one team arrives at the winning site. You are on the winning team.

All the teams gather back at the host home at the end of the event. The small group leader gives a fifteen minute devotion on the human search for our final destination. He congratulates your team for winning and then makes an interesting statement. "The joy you experience in winning this race is temporary. Tomorrow, winning this race will make no difference in your life."

He continues and says, "The things of this earth—like career, possessions, physical pleasure, and sports—provide only temporary happiness." His words about career ring loud and clear. You know that your career is no longer giving you a true sense of purpose. He then invites everyone present to go on a journey, guided by the church's pastor through a message series to some destination points that lead to joy that lasts. You can't wait to hear what the pastor has to say. You hope that he will help you discover a way to experience joy in life.

THE JOURNEY

Life is a journey. The goal of the church is to assist people as they travel from one destination point to the next, and help them move closer to God. This was illustrated by the Strategy Map in chapter four. We are to lead the seeker to be saved and the saved to become servants. Specific destination points were also identified on the map. This portion of the map is illustrated below:

Location Points Along
the Journey Toward Servanthood

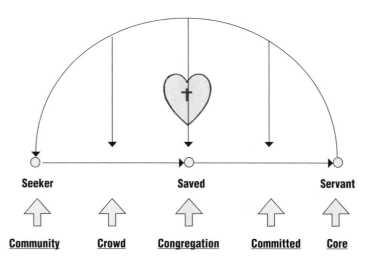

Seeker		Saved		Servant
Community	Crowd	Congregation	Committed	Core

The previous chapter defined the community, crowd, congregation, committed, and core location points found along this path. We find people at each of these location points. Those at the "community" location point are living in the ministry area of the church and are seeking answers for life. A missionary who serves as a church planter in North America recently said that North America is the third largest unreached continent in the world. In our country and around our world, many do not know Christ.

The ministry functions we listed under the "Community" location point (chapter four) are performed to reach people in the community. The church must understand this group of people to be effective in the events it plans. We discover those who are at this location point by leading Ministry Partners to identify people who are in their circles of influence and do not know Christ. These people are invited to attend Intentionally Evangelistic Events (I.E.E.s).

MAPPING THE COMMUNITY

The Strategy Map provides a way for us to plot the location points of people. We use the "Community" location point as a place to write down the names of people who need Christ. For example, let's go back to the story at the beginning of this chapter. Let's say that ten people from the church sit down together and begin to list people who are in their circles of influence and do not know Christ. They write their names under the community location point, and the church targets these people for ministry. This is illustrated in the following diagram:

The Strategy People Map— Mapping the Community

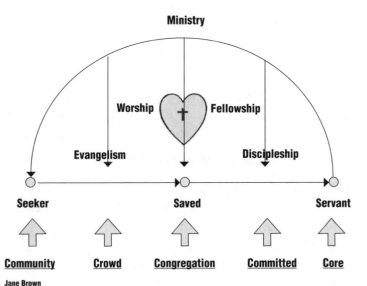

MAPPING THE CROWD

Church members faithfully pray for this group during the month before the event. All the members are able to bring an unsaved or unchurched guest to the event, and there is great excitement. After the event, the Mission Control Leadership team meets and begins to map all the guests who attended. They identify those who attended the event under the "crowd" location point by writing an "E" to signify that they have attended a church-sponsored event. The map is illustrated in the following diagram:

The Strategy People Map—Mapping the Crowd

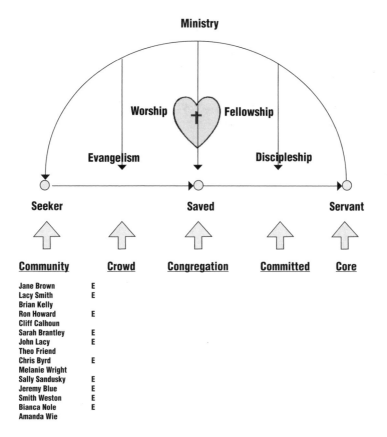

Notice that some who were invited did not attend the event. They continue to be unreached, and church members should continue to pray for them and seek ways to introduce them to Christ. Those who came to the event are now in the crowd and need help on their journey to the next location point. The church has developed outreach teams, which we introduced in the previous chapter, to make further contact with them.

Once again, the leadership team marks information about these "new friends." All those who have been successfully contacted by the outreach team have the "OT" (abbreviation for "Outreach Team" contact) placed by the "E." The outreach teams invited these new friends to attend worship, an open small group called L.I.F.E. Groups, the pastor's guest reception, and the First Steps Training Class. Those who have attended these events are designated with abbreviations designating these events: "W" for "Worship, "LG" for "L.I.F.E. Group," "GR" for "Guest Reception," and "FS" for "First Steps." This is illustrated in "The Strategy Map—Mapping Outreach Contacts" diagram. All of these activities are mapped under our strategy to identify ministries that can be performed to reach individuals at specific location points.

The Strategy Map—Mapping Outreach Contacts

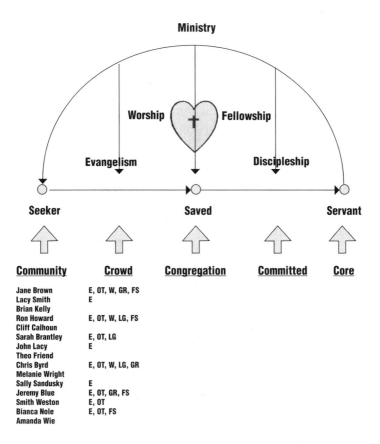

The map reveals that Jane Brown has been contacted by the outreach team (OT) and has attended worship (W), the pastor's guest reception (GR) and the First Steps Training class (FS). Also, the diagram shows that the Outreach Team has not successfully contacted all those who are listed. The outreach team continues to make attempts to contact those who were unavailable.

Mapping the Congregation

The outreach team also records other information about the people they contact. Some who are lost may hear the gospel from an outreach team and decide to commit their life to Christ. Others may already be Christians, but unchurched. This is important information for the leadership team. Those who are saved are part of the congregation of the kingdom of God. To signify that they are Christians, a "C" is placed under the "Congregation" location point on the Strategy People Map.

Those who join the church have letter abbreviations following the "C." The "SB" means they are joining the church by salvation and they need to be baptized. The "B" means they have come from a church that does not practice baptism in the same manner as our congregation and they need to be baptized. The "OD" means they have joined our church from another denomination that practices baptism in the same manner as our congregation. The "T" means they have transferred membership into our church from another church of the same denomination. The "FS" signifies participation in the First Steps membership class. All this is illustrated in "The Strategy People Map—Mapping the Congregation" diagram.

The Strategy People Map—
Mapping the Congregation

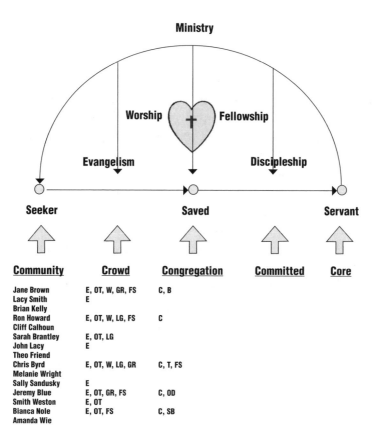

Community	Crowd	Congregation	Committed	Core
Jane Brown	E, OT, W, GR, FS	C, B		
Lacy Smith	E			
Brian Kelly				
Ron Howard	E, OT, W, LG, FS	C		
Cliff Calhoun				
Sarah Brantley	E, OT, LG			
John Lacy	E			
Theo Friend				
Chris Byrd	E, OT, W, LG, GR	C, T, FS		
Melanie Wright				
Sally Sandusky	E			
Jeremy Blue	E, OT, GR, FS	C, OD		
Smith Weston	E, OT			
Bianca Nole	E, OT, FS	C, SB		
Amanda Wie				

The diagram shows that Jane Brown is saved and has joined the church by baptism. This means that she came from a church that does not practice baptism in the same manner as our congregation and needs to be baptized. Ron Howard is a Christian. This was discovered by the outreach team. He has not yet joined the church. Chris Byrd is a Christian and has joined the church by transferring his membership from another church in the same denomination. Jeremy Blue is a Christian and has joined the church from another denomination that practices baptism in the same manner as our congregation. Bianca Nole is a Christian. She recently accepted Christ as her Savior and needs to be baptized. The "B" which designates a need for baptism is changed to bold after the person has been baptized.

MAPPING THE COMMITTED

The next task is to lead people to the "Committed" location point, where believers are involved in small groups. Seekers may attend small groups, but their approach to the group is much different. They are trying to discover who God is and if they want to commit their lives to Him. The diagram shows that Sarah Brantley falls into this category. The believer, however, is in the small group to mature in his faith, and this requires a higher level of commitment than attending worship services only. The small group leader will want to encourage Christians in their group to practice the disciplines of their faith. This includes spending time with God in personal devotion through Bible reading and prayer.

Believers can be in an open small group (L.I.F.E. Group) or a closed small group or both. Open small groups, as defined in chapter three, fulfill the same purposes as the church as a whole. Closed small groups are for believers only and are used to train believers in spiritual maturity issues or in performing ministry. We call these groups "Personal Development" groups, and they are identified through the "CG" (Closed Group) abbreviation.

We also want to record involvement in our training classes, something we have already seen with our First Steps Training Class (FS). A person may take this before he becomes a member of the church (mapped under the "Crowd") or after he becomes a member (mapped under the "Congregation"). The designation for our spiritual gifts class called "Finding Your SHAPE in Ministry" uses the abbreviation SG for "spiritual gifts." The designation for our evangelism class called "How to Share Your Faith" uses the abbreviation EC for "evangelism class." Involvement in these training classes can be seen in the illustration below:

The Strategy People Map—
Mapping the Committee

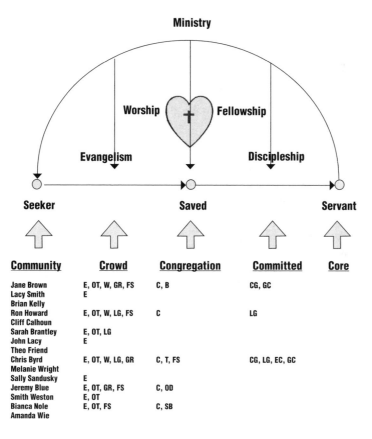

Community	Crowd	Congregation	Committed	Core
Jane Brown	E, OT, W, GR, FS	C, B	CG, GC	
Lacy Smith	E			
Brian Kelly				
Ron Howard	E, OT, W, LG, FS	C	LG	
Cliff Calhoun				
Sarah Brantley	E, OT, LG			
John Lacy	E			
Theo Friend				
Chris Byrd	E, OT, W, LG, GR	C, T, FS	CG, LG, EC, GC	
Melanie Wright				
Sally Sandusky	E			
Jeremy Blue	E, OT, GR, FS	C, OD		
Smith Weston	E, OT			
Bianca Nole	E, OT, FS	C, SB		
Amanda Wie				

The map reveals that Jane Brown is in a closed group and Ron Howard is in a L.I.F.E. Group. Chris Byrd is in both a closed group and a L.I.F.E. Group, and he has taken the Evangelism and Spiritual Gifts classes.

THE SPIRITUAL ASSESSMENT

The leaders of small groups have the great opportunity to help individuals develop spiritually. Leaders are more effective in their ministry to students in a small group when they understand the spiritual condition of their Christian members. However, leaders often treat group members as if they are all on the same spiritual level. The most widely used measurement of spirituality is the frequency of attendance. While this can communicate a message about the spiritual condition of group members, it does not adequately define their spiritual condition.

We have developed a Spiritual Assessment (Appendix A) that allows the leader of a small group to learn about participants in four distinct areas that are related to purpose. The assessment is divided into statements on the following:

1. Love (Loving)—focus is on what we worship and with whom we fellowship.

2. Evangelism (Winning)—focus is on the sharing of our faith.

3. Discipleship (Building)—focus is on our commitments to personal spiritual growth.

4. Ministry (Caring)—focus is on our involvement in meeting the needs of others.

The answers from the assessment are charted on a spider graph. Students are asked to rate themselves using a scale from 0 to 10: "0" meaning that the student has had no success related to the statement, and "10" meaning the student has had complete success related to the statement. All statements have a Scriptural foundation. The process of graphing gives a snapshot of where people are spiritually. Information from the graph is of great importance to individuals who complete the assessment. It shows areas of strength that they can sharpen and areas of weakness that they can address with greater

resolve. The following diagram reflects the spiritual assessment of someone who is strong in the area of caring, which
is aimed toward people in the church. It reveals a weakness in
the area of Evangelism (Winning).

The Spiritual Assessment Spider Graph

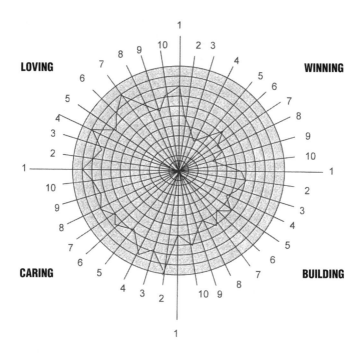

MAPPING THE CORE

Finally, leaders can map the ministry involvement of people
within the church. Those who begin to use their spiritual gifts
in ministry are classified by their ministry focus, the location
points at which their ministry is aimed. Community ministries, designated on the map by number "1," are aimed at
the lost and unchurched in our immediate community and

in our world. Crowd ministries, designated on the map by number "2," are composed of outreach teams. Congregation ministries, designated on the map by number "3," are aimed at helping believers worship and connect to the church family. Committed ministries, designated on the map by number "4," are ministries that help people grow in their faith as believers. These ministries occur through our small groups. We define the ministry involvement of ministry partners by using these numbers on the map under the "Core" identification point. This is illustrated in the following diagram:

The Strategy People Map—Mapping the Core

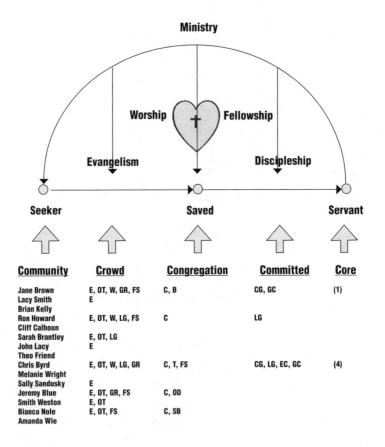

Community	Crowd	Congregation	Committed	Core
Jane Brown	E, OT, W, GR, FS	C, B	CG, GC	(1)
Lacy Smith	E			
Brian Kelly				
Ron Howard	E, OT, W, LG, FS	C	LG	
Cliff Calhoun				
Sarah Brantley	E, OT, LG			
John Lacy	E			
Theo Friend				
Chris Byrd	E, OT, W, LG, GR	C, T, FS	CG, LG, EC, GC	(4)
Melanie Wright				
Sally Sandusky	E			
Jeremy Blue	E, OT, GR, FS	C, OD		
Smith Weston	E, OT			
Bianca Nole	E, OT, FS	C, SB		
Amanda Wie				

The diagram reveals that Jane Brown is involved in a "Community" ministry. She assists in planning I.E.E.s for the Women's Ministry segment of the church. Chris Byrd is involved in a "Committed" ministry. He is serving as a L.I.F.E. Group leader.

MEASURING SUCCESS

The strategy map is helpful because it is measurable, a scoreboard to determine our success. It reveals how well we are doing in ministry to people at each location point. The illustrations below show how the strategy map can be used. The numbers on the scoreboard can be compared to goals that have been set in each area of ministry. Although the numbers shown are from a fairly large congregation, the process of measuring results works the same way in a church of any size.

We can determine how many people are in our "Community" by recording the population in our ministry area. We can measure our "Crowd" ministries by determining how many people have made a connection to our church at intentionally evangelistic events or in worship services or open small groups. We can evaluate "Congregation" ministries by recording how many new members (NM) become part of the church, the total membership (TM) of the church, and the worship attendance (WA) in the church. We can measure the "Committed" ministries by the number of Christians who are involved in small group ministries. And we can evaluate the "Core" ministries by recording how many are part of ministry teams in the church.

Churches of all sizes can better understand their health by mapping the work of the church as a whole. The illustrated church had a beginning membership of 1,250, a beginning average worship attendance of 800, a beginning small group attendance of 700, and a beginning ministry team involvement of 250. The diagram below shows how these numbers have changed over a period of one year.

The Scoreboard of a Healthy Church

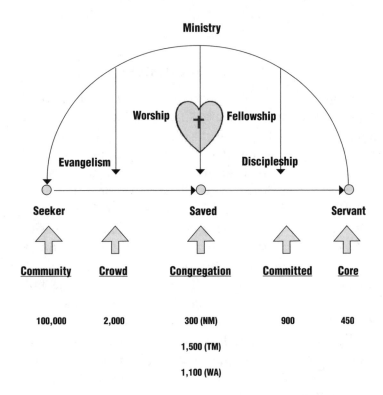

Community	Crowd	Congregation	Committed	Core
100,000	2,000	300 (NM)	900	450
		1,500 (TM)		
		1,100 (WA)		

- There are 100,000 people in the community reached by the church.

- The church has made connection with 2,000 people, who are now part of the "Crowd."

- Of the 2,000 who have been reached, three hundred have joined the church and are part of the "Congregation."

- There are now 1,500 total members in the "Congregation."

- On average, 1,100 people attend worship as "Congregation" members.

- Nine hundred believers are in a small group and are classified as "Committed."

- Four hundred fifty people have a ministry in the church, and they make up the "Core" of the church. This represents 30 percent of the congregation, an increase from 20 percent recorded the previous year.

The above diagram illustrates a healthy church that is becoming more balanced in its approach to ministry. Look at the following diagram, which reveals the measurement points of another church in the same area. It had the same beginning membership of 1,250, beginning worship attendance of 800, a beginning small group attendance of 700, and a beginning ministry team membership of 250. Again, the diagram shows the ministry activity during a period of one year.

The Scoreboard of an Unhealthy Church

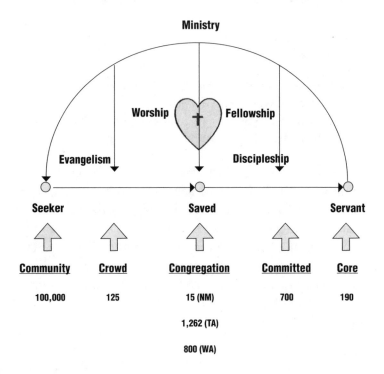

- There are 100,000 people in the community reached by the church.

- The church has made connection with 125 people, who are now part of the "Crowd."

- Of the 125 who have been reached, fifteen have joined the church and are part of the "Congregation."

- There are now 1,262 total members in the "Congregation."

- On average, 800 people attend worship as "Congregation" members.

- Seven hundred believers are in a small group and are classified as "Committed."

- One hundred ninety people have a ministry in the church, and they make up the "Core" of the church. This represents 15 percent of the congregation, a decrease from 20 percent recorded the previous year.

Let's look at these numbers a little more closely. The diagram reveals that the church connected with only 125 new friends in a community of 100,000 people during the year. There are some possible causes for this. First, there may not be enough emphasis on personal evangelism. Second, they may not be planning ministry activities to reach the lost. Third, their worship services may not be sensitive to non-believers and may therefore be confusing to people who are lost. The problem may be a combination of these three causes.

Notice that only fifteen people joined the church during the year. This increased the church membership to a total of 1,262 members. The diagram also reveals that the worship attendance and the small group attendance stayed the same. This is due to the lack of new members coming into the church. Common sense tells us that if the number of non-believers who attend church ministries is smaller, the number of potential new believers will be smaller.

Finally, you will notice that the number of ministry team members decreased to 190. This represents 15 percent of the church membership, a decrease from the previous year's 20 percent. This reveals that the church was unsuccessful at leading people to the destination God desires—becoming His servants—and that some who are involved are losing their motivation to serve. A possible reason for this is the church's lack of focus to reach the lost, disciple believers, and involve maturing believers in ministry.

This church is in danger of becoming an inward-focused church, with members who are more interested in their own needs than the needs of others. Two signs point to this problem. First, there is a lack of evangelism in the church. Second, there has been a reduction in the number of volunteer ministers in the church. This must be corrected or the church will crash. Volunteer ministry increases when reaching the lost becomes a priority of the church and members understand the importance of their service. A church that serves God serves others.

Are you willing to make the effort to define purpose, paint the picture, develop the plan, and give your people a part to play? Are you willing to lead people to God's desired destination?

6

THE PARTICIPATION

It was he who gave some to be apostles, some to be prophets, some to be evangelists, and some to be pastors and teachers, to prepare God's people for works of service, so that the body of Christ may be built up until we all reach unity in the faith and in the knowledge of the Son of God and become mature, attaining to the whole measure of the fullness of Christ.

—EPHESIANS 4:11–13

Defining the Roles of Key Leaders in the Church

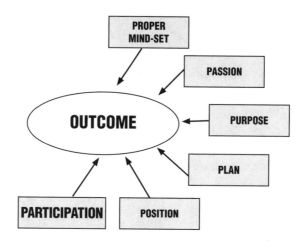

What a race! The event, called The Red Bull Divide and Conquer, was held in June 2004. The relay race consisted of teams passing a silver rock between four contestants who used their expertise in running, paragliding, kayaking, and biking. The course was set within the San Juan Mountain range along the Continental Divide. The terrain is rugged, ranging from 7,000 to 13,000 feet, and poses a great challenge for each team. To complete the course requires the efforts of skilled individuals with expertise in specific areas who are willing to use their talents as they work together as a team.

How would you like to compete alone in a race like this? I can't see myself competing in one leg of the race, much less trying it solo. My previous concept of relay races was that athletes, all having similar talents and abilities, ran around a track and passed off a stick to another runner with a set of fresh legs. However, I believe the Divide and Conquer race is a much better description of church ministry. Church leaders relay people (not a silver rock) to the next leader who possesses certain talents and abilities. Just as the athletes in the Divide and Conquer competition had different talents and abilities, leaders in the church also have different strengths.

As church leaders, we face a difficult terrain. We face an enemy who longs for our failure. He has a different take on "Divide and Conquer." His goal is to divide us so that he can conquer us. Our enemy's method of making war is not new. We have seen it in past wars, and we see it today in our new battle with terrorists who use the strategy of turning citizens of the same country against one another. Satan uses a similar strategy against the church. He works to turn believers against one another, to keep us from working together to advance God's kingdom. And this strategy works. Church after church has experienced division, and people miss heaven as a result. He influences us to become turf protectors or to concentrate on our own needs rather than the needs of others. War is the result.

How can this be overcome? We overcome division in the church by focusing on the ministry God has called us to perform. He has called us to reach out to others with the good news. The early church in the New Testament experienced a great unity of spirit. The Bible says, "Every day they continued to meet together in the temple courts. They broke bread in their homes and ate together with glad and sincere hearts, praising God and enjoying the favor of all the people. And the Lord added to their number daily those who were being saved" (Acts 2:46– 47). Doesn't this sound like a great church? They were able to maintain unity by focusing their attention on leading people to experience the saving power of Jesus Christ, and on serving the community of God.

George Barna wrote:

> I am convinced that if the typical unchurched person were invited to get involved with such a collection of believers—people engaged in the kind of life described in these few verses—they would jump at the opportunity. And why shouldn't everyone have the chance? [3]

A Relay Ministry

A healthy church operates by a "relay ministry." In the process of moving people closer to God, leaders pass off people to other leaders who have expertise in certain areas. This is God's idea of "divide and conquer." We are to divide the responsibilities of ministry among ministry partners who are gifted in certain areas, and allow them to use their gifts in moving people closer to God. The "divide and conquer" approach allows us to succeed in leading others to become servants of God. The Strategy Map shows us how this is accomplished.

The diagram shows the purposes—worship, fellowship, evangelism, discipleship, and ministry—and uses directional arrows to illustrate people moving from one location to the next. Notice that each action of purpose related to these arrows has the name of a leader adjacent to the ministry action. The names appear in bold lettering.

The Strategy Map—a Relay Ministry

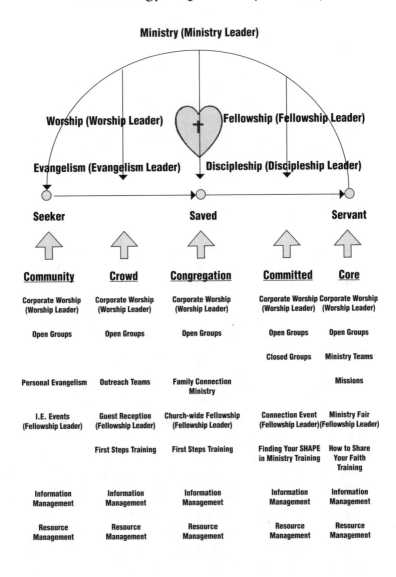

Ministry (Ministry Leader)

Worship (Worship Leader) Fellowship (Fellowship Leader)

Evangelism (Evangelism Leader) Discipleship (Discipleship Leader)

Seeker   Saved   Servant

Community	Crowd	Congregation	Committed	Core
Corporate Worship (Worship Leader)	Corporate Worship (Worship Leader)	Corporate Worship (Worship Leader)	Corporate Worship (Worship Leader)	Corporate Worship (Worship Leader)
Open Groups	Open Groups	Open Groups	Open Groups	Open Groups
			Closed Groups	Ministry Teams
Personal Evangelism	Outreach Teams	Family Connection Ministry		Missions
I.E. Events (Fellowship Leader)	Guest Reception (Fellowship Leader)	Church-wide Fellowship (Fellowship Leader)	Connection Event (Fellowship Leader)	Ministry Fair (Fellowship Leader)
	First Steps Training	First Steps Training	Finding Your SHAPE in Ministry Training	How to Share Your Faith Training
Information Management	Information Management	Information Management	Information Management	Information Management
Resource Management	Resource Management	Resource Management	Resource Management	Resource Management

THE EVANGELISM LEADER

The Evangelism Leader should have a passion for the unsaved. He and those who serve with him in the ministry of leading seekers to be saved should be passionate about evangelism. It is his responsibility to make certain that all the ministry actions under the "Community" and "Crowd" location points take place. He recruits leaders who are gifted in planning events for the lost and who are also gifted in building relationships with those who do not know Christ. The Evangelism Leader should work closely with the Worship Leadership to ensure that evangelism is a strategic part of the worship experience. He is responsible for encouraging ministry partners to complete the "Winning—How to Share Your Faith" class, offered as a closed group course.

As he works with intentionally evangelistic events (I.E.E.s), the Evangelism Leader realizes that success in reaching the lost is dependent upon church members cultivating relationships with people in their circles of influence. He works closely with the fellowship leader to conduct I.E.E.s and guest events, making certain that all resources are available for the events. Depending on the size of the church, the evangelism leader may develop a leadership team based on the ministry activities. The smaller the church, the more responsibility he will need to take in each area. Those who are reached through the evangelism ministry of the church are "relayed" to the next leader.

The Discipleship Leader

The Discipleship Leader should have passion for spiritual growth. He has the responsibility for all ministry activities found under the "Congregation" and the "Committed" location points. The discipleship leader will work with the worship leader to make certain that discipleship themes are a priority in worship experiences. He will oversee the open and closed small group ministries, and he will also work with the fellowship leader to conduct church-wide fellowships and connection events. This leader may also develop a leadership team centered on ministry activities. Again, the smaller the church, the more responsibility the leader will take in each area. Those who mature in this ministry are "relayed" to the next leader.

The Ministry Leader

The Ministry Leader should have a passion for serving others. He has the responsibility of involving ministry partners in ministry. As he teaches the "Building—Finding Your SHAPE in Ministry" class, he discovers the interests and spiritual gifts of class participants and relays information to ministry team leaders within the church. The ministry team leaders then make contact with the new ministry volunteers and find ways to involve them in ministry. The ministry leader must maintain good communication with other leaders to become aware of ministry related needs. He also has the responsibility of developing a directory of ministry positions in the church. This is a tool used to communicate ministry opportunities within the church.

The Worship Leader

The Worship Leader should have a passion for helping others connect with God. He works with the evangelism leader, the discipleship leader, and the ministry leader to make certain that themes related to their areas of ministry are emphasized in weekly corporate worship or through special worship events throughout the year. He is also responsible to plan weekly corporate worship experiences that meet the needs of the different people groups in the church.

The Fellowship Leader

The Fellowship Leader should have a passion for helping people connect with others. He is responsible to work with the evangelism leader, the discipleship leader, and the ministry leader to conduct fellowship events that assist them in their areas of ministry. They coordinate efforts to make certain that all resources are secured, including facilities and food products.

You may be saying, "Tim, our church doesn't have five staff ministers to do this." The good news is that you don't need five ministers on staff. Our church has not always been the size we are today, and we haven't always had a large staff. In fact, our staff is small compared to other churches our size. The strategy works in smaller churches through the participation of volunteers who have a passion for certain areas of ministry. Smaller churches can effectively use volunteers because they have fewer contacts to make. The larger the church, the more people there are, and the greater the need for professional ministry personnel. Resources to hire ministry personnel become available as the church reaches more people.

OPEN SMALL GROUP LEADERSHIP

The open small group ministry is one of the most important ministries in the church. We call our open small groups "L.I.F.E. Groups." These groups provide an opportunity for community within the church, and all ministry partners are encouraged to participate in a group. Ministry partners who are members of a group feel like they are part of the church family no matter how large the church becomes. We tell people that our church is growing smaller as we grow larger. In other words, we are adding new small groups as the church grows larger, so people have opportunities to make connection in the church.

Open small groups, as we have previously learned, perform the same functions as the church. They fulfill the purposes of evangelism, discipleship, ministry, worship, and fellowship. Open Small Groups are truly little churches. We have organized our Open Small Group Leadership Teams with the same strategy as that used by the church. This is illustrated in the following diagram:

The Open Small Group Strategy

Ministry (Ministry Leader)

Worship   Fellowship

Evangelism (Evangelism Leader)   Discipleship (Discipleship Leader)

Seeker   Saved   Servant

Community	Crowd	Congregation	Committed	Core
Personal Evangelism	Outreach Teams	Teaching Ministry	Spiritual Assessment	Care System
I E Events			Spiritual Growth Plan	Target Ministry
Information Management	Information Management	Information Management	Information Management	Information Management
Resource Management	Resource Management	Resource Management	Resource Management	Resource Management

Notice that the Evangelism Leader (we call him the "Winning Leader") in the L.I.F.E. Group is responsible for "Community" and "Crowd" activities. He encourages people in building relationships with the lost and inviting them to events that will help them connect with the group. He is also responsible for organizing outreach teams to make further contact with those who have attended I.E.E.s.

The Discipleship Leader (we call him the "Building Leader") is responsible for the "Congregation" and "Committed" ministry activities. He develops a teaching plan that addresses the spiritual needs of group participants. To help with this, he must lead believers in the class to complete the spiritual assessment discussed in chapter five. (It is included in this book as Appendix A.) The completed assessment will give him needed information for his teaching plans. The discipleship leader encourages believers in the group to daily spend time with God through involvement in a Spiritual Growth Plan. This plan helps students practice the disciplines of their faith (Bible study, meditation, Scripture memory, and prayer) and daily journal their quiet time with God.

The Ministry Leader (we call him the "Caring Leader") has the responsibility of encouraging students to be involved in acts of ministry. He plans ministry opportunities by leading the group to adopt a Target Ministry, a local social ministry that needs volunteers. A target ministry may be a local soup kitchen, a regional children's home, an air-flight ministry, a clothing ministry, or a pregnancy center. This leader also organizes a care ministry to meet the needs of members in the group.

The Winning Leader, the Building Leader, and the Caring Leader make up the nucleus of the leadership team. They are responsible to lead the seekers to be saved and the saved to become servants. The cell group is made up of members who are identified as seekers, the saved, and servants. This is illustrated in the following diagram:

The L.I.F.E. Group Cell (Open Small Group)

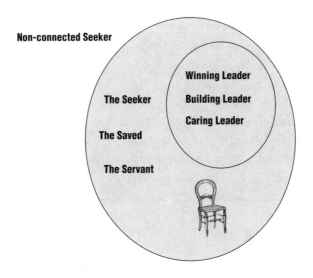

This diagram also highlights the non-connected seeker who is outside the cell. Leaders work to fill the empty chair in the cell group with the non-connected seeker.

CONNECTING CHURCH LEADERS TO OPEN SMALL GROUP LEADERS

The evangelism minister/leader of the church assists the "Winning Leaders" in the L.I.F.E. Groups with training, planning, and accountability. The discipleship leader provides the "Building Leader" in the L.I.F.E. Group with training, teaching resources, spiritual assessment resources, and spiritual growth plan resources, which may include devotional materials, quiet time guides, and prayer guides. The ministry leader helps the "Caring Leader" in the L.I.F.E. Group by communicating information about ministry positions in the church and possible target ministries in the community, and by encouraging him to involve the small group members in spiritual gift training. The goal of our L.I.F.E. Groups is to lead people to become servants. The more servants we have, the more lost people we will reach and the more groups we will need.

Our small groups are cell groups that meet both on campus and off campus. The decision to conduct off-campus groups was twofold. First, we ran out of space on campus. Second, we wanted to take these groups into the mission field. We have discovered that many who are lost will not step foot on the church campus for a worship service, but they will come to a home for fellowship and a Bible study on a relevant topic.

We don't judge the lost for their unwillingness to come to a worship experience. Our ministry partners have learned to not expect the lost to act like they are saved. We are more concerned with reaching them where they are and leading them to Christ. The more they get to know the people in the group, the more willing they are to attend worship events. Every Sunday worship service becomes an I.E.E. for an off-campus group.

Our desire is that open small groups multiply annually. However, this does not always occur. Many of the campus groups that do not multiply do not grow because they are not conducting I.E.E.s. Groups that meet on campus must conduct these events to reach the lost. An event is an I.E.E. if lost and/or unchurched people attend. Otherwise, it's just a Christian fellowship. The groups in our church that grow without these events are growing with Christian people who have visited or joined our church. This sense of growth gives group leaders and members a false sense of success. Giving believers a place for community is important, but leading believers to love a lost world and to reach those in the world is critical.

The exciting part of our L.I.F.E. Group ministry is that they are generating new friends. The church begins to expand its reach quickly when the church as a whole, open small groups, and ministry segments are all intentionally connecting with those who need Christ.

MINISTRY SEGMENT LEADERSHIP

A ministry segment is a ministry aimed at a people group, a particular segment of the population. Ministry segments include children's ministry, youth ministry, singles ministry, young married without children ministry, young married with children ministry, middle-aged adult ministry with no children, middle-aged adult ministry with young children, middle-aged adult ministry with youth, senior adult ministry, language ministries, special needs ministries...and the list goes on. The leader over a people group is responsible to fulfill the purposes of evangelism, discipleship, and ministry worship and fellowship. Each segment group "relays" or passes people from one leader to the next to assist them as they move closer to God.

The church strategy map also applies to these groups. For example, look at the following figure illustrating the youth segment ministry. The youth minister has responsibility over a youth evangelism leader, a youth discipleship leader, a youth ministry leader, a youth worship leader, and a youth fellowship leader.

The Strategy Map for the Youth Segment Ministry

Ministry (Ministry Leader)

Worship (Worship Leader) **Fellowship (Fellowship Leader)**

Evangelism (Evangelism Leader) **Discipleship (Discipleship Leader)**

Seeker   **Saved**   **Servant**

Community	Crowd	Congregation	Committed	Core
Youth Worship (Worship Leader)	Youth Worship (Worship Leader)	Youth Worship (Worship Leader)	Youth Worship (Worship Leader)	Youth Worship (Worship Leader)
Open Groups	Open Groups	Open Groups	Open Groups	Open Groups
			Closed Groups	Ministry Teams
Personal Evangelism	Outreach Teams			Missions
I.E. Events (Fellowship Leader)	Guest Reception (Fellowship Leader)	Youth Fellowship (Fellowship Leader)	Connection Event (Fellowship Leader)	Ministry Fair (Fellowship Leader)
	First Steps Training	First Steps Training	Finding Your SHAPE in Ministry Training	How to Share Your Faith Training
Information Management	Information Management	Information Management	Information Management	Information Management
Resource Management	Resource Management	Resource Management	Resource Management	Resource Management

The evangelism leader of a youth ministry has the responsibility of encouraging and training students to become personal evangelists. He provides tools for inviting students to I.E.E.'s that are created to target the youth of our culture. Students may go to an amusement park, have a sumo wrestling night, go to a concert, or go skiing. This only scratches the surface. These events generate new friends for the church, and the evangelism leader sends outreach teams to their homes to build further relationships with them and share the good news of Christ. The leader ensures that information on the new students is recorded. He also plans fellowship events that encourage them to connect with others in the group.

The discipleship leader of a youth ministry develops a teaching plan that is relevant to the spiritual needs of students. He also determines the target audience of L.I.F.E. Groups that function within the youth ministry and may be organized around age, gender, geography, interest, or a variety of other categories. He is responsible for creating a closed group training program that will train students in evangelism, discipleship, and ministry.

The ministry leader involves students in a ministry plan for service to those inside the segment group and mission to those outside of the group. This may be through a care system of ministry aimed at group members or missions opportunities aimed at local social ministries, state missions projects, national missions projects, or international missions projects.

The worship leader oversees the corporate worship experiences for students. These may occur weekly, monthly, or seasonally. He works with other leaders to promote special themes during worship experiences.

The fellowship leader joins with the evangelism leader, the discipleship leader, and the ministry leader to plan and conduct fellowship events. He makes certain that resources are in place for these events.

The strategy map is used to organize activities for each ministry segment. It also unites all the ministries of the church as they use a common strategy to accomplish the purposes of the church and assist people as they move closer to God.

Our segment ministries use this strategy to ensure that they are developing servants of God. It is also used to hold segment ministry leaders accountable for their work. The pastor can identify planned ministry activities at each location point and evaluate their success by requiring segment leaders to map the people they reach through their ministry (See section on mapping in chapter five).

WINNING THE RACE

We can win the race if we keep our eyes on the prize. The apostle Paul wrote:

> Do you not know that in a race all the runners run, but only one gets the prize? Run in such a way as to get the prize. Everyone who competes in the games goes into strict training. They do it to get a crown that will not last; but we do it to get a crown that will last forever. Therefore I do not run like a man running aimlessly; I do not fight like a man beating the air. No, I beat my body and make it my slave so that after I have preached to others, I myself will not be disqualified for the prize.
> —1 CORINTHIANS 9:24–27

Paul went through strict training to prepare himself for the ministry of preaching the gospel. As church leaders we have the responsibility of training others to run the race. We are to train believers to become servants who direct others toward the ultimate prize of eternal life. We are not running aimlessly. We are in strict training to prepare to be workmen who please God. The desire of every leader must be to effectively fulfill his role in the relay, leading others to the ultimate destination of becoming servants of God.

7

THE PERSON

Those who live according to the sinful nature have their minds set on what that nature desires; but those who live in accordance with the Spirit have their minds set on what the Spirit desires. The mind of sinful man is death, but the mind controlled by the Spirit is life and peace; the sinful mind is hostile to God. It does not submit to God's law, nor can it do so. Those controlled by the sinful nature cannot please God. You, however, are controlled not by the sinful nature but by the Spirit, if the Spirit of God lives in you.

—ROMANS 8:5–9

Becoming an Effective Leader

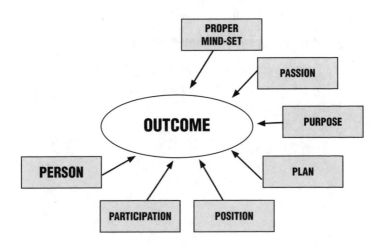

The hot Florida sun is shining brightly with no clouds in sight as you wait your turn to tee up a little white dimpled ball. You're not the greatest golfer in the world, but becoming a pastor has been quite helpful to your game. You normally play with church members, which means that you can no longer throw golf clubs, scream, or pick up your ball in anger and throw it in the lake. Now you must show patience and control your frustration. You've discovered that the golf course has a funny way of revealing a person's true character, even yours.

You wonder what this hole will bring. Success requires a long shot with your driver down the middle of the fairway. If you miss the fairway, those large sand-filled bunkers are to the right and the left. If you hit it too long, water from the lake comes into play. You hit the ball, and miraculously it stays just on the right side of the fairway, a perfect location for your next shot to the green.

The decisions become more difficult now. Choosing the driver off of the tee was a no-brainer. You love the driver. Now you must decide which iron to use. This is difficult because you never seem to hit your irons the same way twice. You are about 100 yards from the green and know that if you hit your 9 iron smoothly, you'll be right on the hole. The problem is you only hit your irons smoothly about 20 percent of the time. You must decide whether to compensate for past failures and choose an 8 iron instead, hoping that you don't hit it perfectly. If you do, you'll hit the ball 10 yards past the green and into the woods. You decide to play your 9 iron and hope for an awesome shot. You swing, and to your great astonishment, you're on the green just 10 feet from the hole. The fun begins.

You now have the great privilege of using your putter, the dreaded putter. The good news is that you haven't purposely broken a putter since you became a pastor. The bad news is that you disposed of three before you became a pastor. You hate the putter, as though it was to blame that the ball always seems to miss the hole. The pressure is on. You put...

The purpose of this chapter is to begin developing in leaders and church members the qualities that are necessary for success. Understanding your purpose, having a plan, and knowing how to determine the position of people in the church is not enough. Poor leadership causes instability in the church. John Maxwell, a noted author and speaker in the area of business and church leadership, wrote: "No matter how hard you work, you can only go so far professionally if you are a poor leader. A company, department, or team will always be held back by a weak leader."[1] This also applies to the organization called "the church." Four influential components affect the leader's ability to influence others to accomplish a stated purpose. These are illustrated in the following diagram, and they will be the concentration of this chapter.

The Leadership Diamond

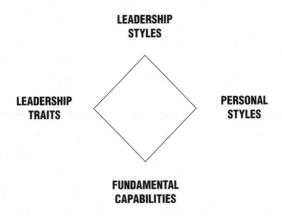

The Skill of Choosing Leadership Styles

Choosing which golf club to use on the golf course is similar to choosing a leadership style. The situation dictates the leadership style that is needed. Daniel Goleman, a professor at

Harvard, taught about the importance of choosing the appropriate leadership style for a given situation in an article in the *Harvard Business Review*. He wrote:

> …the research indicates that leaders with the best results do not rely on only one leadership style; they use most of them in a given week—seamlessly and in different measure—depending on the business situation. Imagine the styles, then, as the array of clubs in a golf pro's bag. Over the course of a game, the pro picks and chooses clubs based on the demands of the shot.[2]

Are you a pro, or are you like the golfer who has a difficult time deciding what club to use? Consider how ridiculous it would be for a golfer to use his driver on every shot, whether he was far from the green, close to the green, or on the green. Yet some church leaders use the same leadership style in every situation, even when it is inappropriate.

Healthy churches have leaders who understand their predominant leadership styles and are adept at using all leadership styles when it is necessary. Developing a plan for ministry is not enough to experience success in the church. Leaders will not succeed if they destroy the morale of people along the way, and this frequently occurs when they use an inappropriate leadership style in a given situation. The ability of leaders in this area can have a direct effect on the outcome of ministry within the church.

LEADERSHIP STYLES

Goleman lists six leadership styles, defines them, and details situations that are appropriate for their use. As you read the following leadership style definitions, circle the qualities that describe you.

1. *The Authoritative (Visionary) Leader.* He leads people toward a vision. The style works best when

an organization needs a new vision or when a clear direction is needed.

2. *The Coercive Leader*. He demands immediate compliance from others. The style works best when in a crisis, to kick-start a turnaround, or with problem employees.

3. *The Affiliative Leader*. He creates harmony and builds emotional bonds. The style works best to heal rifts in a team or to motivate people during stressful circumstances.

4. *The Democratic Leader*. He forges consensus through participation. The style works best to build buy-in or consensus, or to get input from valuable employees.

5. *The Pacesetting Leader*. He is driven to achieve and sets high standards for performance. The style works best to get quick results from a highly motivated and competent team.

6. *The Coaching Leader*. He develops people for the future by investing time in them. The style works best to help an employee improve performance or develop long-term strengths.[3]

You have most likely been able to identify your predominant leadership style by reading these definitions. Do you use this style most of the time, or do you change styles according to the situation? Each style has its place in ministry. The more professional you become at using these styles, the more successful you will be. The health of the church is dependent on wise leadership style choices by you, the leader.

PERSONAL STYLES

Choosing the right leadership style for a given situation is critical in leading others to accomplish tasks. However, leadership styles are not the only defining qualities that impact our ability to lead. Carlson Learning Systems developed a self-administered assessment tool to determine our predominant personal styles. This assessment is known as the DiSC profile.[4] The acrostic relates to four specific personal styles that are defined below. Circle the words and phrases that best describe you.

DOMINANCE

- Risk takers
- Determined
- Decision maker
- Competitive
- Problem solver
- Productive
- Enjoys challenges
- Goal driven

INTERACTION

- Energetic
- Very verbal
- Spontaneous
- Friendly
- Optimistic
- Thinks out loud
- Popular
- Motivates others

STEADINESS

- Loyal
- Avoids confrontation
- Dislikes change
- Patient
- Sympathetic
- Indecisive
- Sensitive
- Not demanding of others

Cautiousness

- Accurate
- Practical
- Reserved
- Orderly
- Factual
- Likes instructions
- Detailed
- Conscientious

Which of these personal styles best describe you? Understanding your personal style is not enough to experience success as a church leader. We must also master four fundamental capabilities.

The Four Fundamental Capabilities

Understanding predominant leadership styles and personal traits is important because they impact the way we interact with those we lead. Goleman taught that leaders must also consider what he calls "emotional intelligence." He wrote that emotional intelligence is "the ability to manage ourselves and our relationships effectively."[5]

Those who come from a secular background attempt to control their emotions through self effort. We as believers know that our emotions and outward behavior come from the attitudes of our hearts. Leaders who act harshly toward ministry partners or others on the leadership team have a heart problem. Leaders should always treat people with the love of God, regardless of the circumstance. Unfortunately, I have been witness to many church situations where leaders did not show this love. I was guilty of this myself early in my ministry. This behavior comes from a self-centered attitude. Church leaders are no longer protecting others but themselves when this occurs.

Goleman identified four responsibilities for leaders. They are to "set strategy; motivate; create a mission; and build a culture."[6]

To fulfill these responsibilities leaders must master four areas called the "fundamental capabilities." These capabilities apply to every leader, both in secular and spiritual organizations. They include:

1. Self-Awareness: The self-aware have the ability to read and understand their emotions as well as recognize their impact on work performance, relationships, and the like.[7]

Are you self-aware? I am amazed that some leaders are so clueless about their behavior. They run over someone emotionally and don't even realize what they have done. This is an area of personal conviction for me. I am borderline bi-polar, and I'm either on top of the world or on the bottom. When I am at the top of the world, my enthusiasm assists me greatly as I lead others. However, when I am at the bottom, my neglect of people drives them away from me. Three years ago I hit the bottom and realized the effect I was having on my leadership team. I made a decision to do whatever was necessary to bring change. This continues to be a struggle for me, but, according to my wife, I am much improved. The change began because I became aware of the effect I was having on others. Those who succeed must master self-awareness.

2. Self-Management: Those who practice self-management have the ability to keep disruptive emotions and impulses under control.[8]

Do you practice self-management? The secularist believes that his ability to practice proper self-management comes completely from himself. The believer understands that his ability to accomplish this comes from his faith in God. Peter instructed us to stand "firm in the faith…" (1 Pet. 5:9). The strength of our faith in God affects our behavior. Those who live by faith have a desire to bring glory to God. This desire causes them to manage their lives in a way that directs people toward Him.

The golfer in the opening illustration may not accurately describe you, but it nails me. It was not fun to play golf with me before I became a pastor. I changed when I realized the negative influence I could have by leading people in the congregation away from God and not to Him. Church leaders can quickly lose their ability to positively influence others when they act in an ungodly manner. I have seen this occur on the athletic field and in the stands. Those who behave this way have a heart problem and give evidence that God is not in control. Proper self-management occurs when we live to please God.

3. Social Awareness: The socially aware are skilled at sensing other people's emotions, understanding their perspective, and taking an active interest in their concerns.[9]

Are you socially aware? Do you really care about the needs of people, or do you want to get your way? Ministry is not about getting our way; it is about serving others and leading them to follow God's way. Once again, earlier in my ministry I had the tendency to make decisions that did not take the needs of others into account. For example, I made some decisions that adversely affected the senior adults in our church. This has a name—"pastoral suicide." Two older men, who I have come to greatly appreciate, brought this to my attention. They later became two of my strongest supporters.

Fortunately, many people were coming to know Christ and were joining our church. This was my salvation. However, I had to change my way of thinking to be successful. The previous ten years of my life had been spent in youth ministry. Have you noticed that very few senior adults have youth? My ministry focused on students and their parents. Pastors must be concerned about every group in the church and must consider how their decisions will affect all groups.

4. Social Skill: Those who use proper social skill have the ability to take charge and inspire with a compelling vision through the use of good communication.[10]

Do you have social skill? Do you have the ability to inspire others into action? One of our biggest tasks as church leaders is to coach those under us so that they grow and mature as followers and as potential leaders. To do this, we must be able to effectively communicate, initiate change, deal with conflict, build relationships with others, and develop a ministry team.

We are team builders. God commissions us to train people to do the work of God. The Bible says:

> It was he who gave some to be apostles, some to be prophets, some to be evangelists, and some to be pastors and teachers, to prepare God's people for works of service, so that the body of Christ may be built up until we all reach unity in the faith and in the knowledge of the Son of God and become mature, attaining to the whole measure of the fullness of Christ.
>
> —EPHESIANS 4:11–13

The church quickly becomes unhealthy when we attempt to do all the work ourselves, or when we buy into the idea that the church has hired us to do all the ministries. Our job as ministers is to mobilize the people of the church to use their gifts in acts of service and mission.

LEADERSHIP TRAITS

What is God looking for in a leader? Becoming the leader that God desires is the most critical element of becoming a successful leader. Church leaders should possess certain traits, and we discover these traits in the dialogue that took place between Moses and his father-in-law, Jethro. Moses was trying to do everything himself, and Jethro wanted to help him. Jethro confronted Moses and said:

> What you are doing is not good. You and these people who come to you will only wear yourselves out. The work is too heavy for you; you cannot handle it alone. Listen now to me and I will give you some advice, and may God be with you. You must be the people's representative before God and bring their disputes to him. Teach them the decrees and laws, and show them the way to

live and the duties they are to perform. But select capable men from all the people—men who fear God, trustworthy men who hate dishonest gain—and appoint them as officials over thousands, hundreds, fifties and tens. Have them serve as judges for the people at all times, but have them bring every difficult case to you; the simple cases they can decide themselves. That will make your load lighter, because they will share it with you. If you do this and God so commands, you will be able to stand the strain, and all these people will go home satisfied.

—Exodus 18:17–23

What great advice! This passage includes ten vital leadership traits.

1. *They are capable.* The word *capable* means "having the ability or qualities necessary for."[11] Those selected to lead are to have the abilities and qualities necessary to accomplish the assigned tasks. Do you have the abilities to do your assignment?

2. *They fear God.* The word *fear* means "awe; reverence."[12] Those selected to lead are to be in awe of God. They are to revere Him, having hearts that are committed to Him. Is your heart fully devoted to God?

3. *They are trustworthy.* The word *trustworthy* means "dependable and reliable."[13] Those selected to lead are to be dependable, having the trust of others. Can you be trusted to follow through on your commitments?

4. *They teach others to honor God.* Moses had the responsibility of teaching God's decrees and laws to the people. Those who followed these commands honored Him. Do you base your life on the instruction of God's Word?

5. *They are an example in life.* Moses received guidance that he should show the people the way to live. Are you a godly example in word and in deed?

6. *They teach others how to perform their tasks.* Moses was instructed to show the people the duties they were to perform. Do you train others to do the jobs they have been assigned?

7. *They select other leaders.* Moses received direction to recruit others to help him in his tasks. They were to be capable, they were to fear God, and they were to be trustworthy. Do you recruit other leaders to assist you in ministry? Do they fulfill these requirements?

8. *They appoint others on the basis of their giftedness.* Moses was advised to appoint leaders over thousands, hundred, fifties, and tens. Those who lead groups must have the appropriate spiritual gifts. Do you appoint leaders according to their giftedness?

9. *They resolve conflict.* Moses was available to handle the difficult cases that could not be resolved by those in lower levels of leadership. Do you resolve conflict before it becomes an emergency?

10. *They delegate.* Moses was responsible for handling only the difficult cases. He was not to do the work of those under him. Do you allow people to do the jobs they have been assigned?

Do all these traits describe you? A healthy church has leaders who are defined by these traits. One way to determine if these traits are true of you is to restate them in a personal manner. Complete the following exercise.

LEADERSHIP EXERCISE

Circle the number that best describes your mastery of the following leadership traits. Zero (0) means that you are completely unsuccessful, and 10 means that you are completely successful.

I am capable.

0 1 2 3 4 5 6 7 8 9 10

I fear God.

0 1 2 3 4 5 6 7 8 9 10

I am dependable.

0 1 2 3 4 5 6 7 8 9 10

I teach others to honor God.

0 1 2 3 4 5 6 7 8 9 10

My life is a Godly example for others

0 1 2 3 4 5 6 7 8 9 10

I teach others how to perform their tasks.

0 1 2 3 4 5 6 7 8 9 10

I select others to assist me in ministry.

0 1 2 3 4 5 6 7 8 9 10

I appoint others on the basis of their giftedness.

0 1 2 3 4 5 6 7 8 9 10

I resolve conflict.

0 1 2 3 4 5 6 7 8 9 10

I delegate responsibilities and allow those under me to do their jobs.

0 1 2 3 4 5 6 7 8 9 10

WHERE'S THE BALL?

We ended the opening illustration with a putt. Is it in the hole? Mastering the leadership traits makes you a pro and puts the ball in the center of the cup. If you missed, don't get frustrated with the game and quit. Keep practicing, and learn to be the leader that God desires.

8
THE PROCESS

And whatever you do, whether in word or deed, do it all in the name of the Lord Jesus, giving thanks to God the Father through him.
—COLOSSIANS 3:17

Effective Communication in the Church

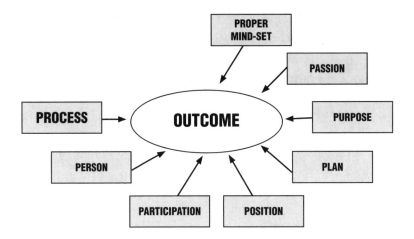

Your career is far from the one your parents had hoped for. They had dreamed that you would become a doctor, a lawyer, or maybe even a teacher. But you discovered your unique gift of making people laugh. You always seemed to be the center of attention at parties and other gatherings. This led you to make a brave decision to become a stand-up comedian. Audiences love you—that is, audiences in America.

You find yourself in a difficult position. You've been asked to tour England and your first gig is a huge failure. Your jokes seem to die in mid air, and the audience is silent except for one American guy in the back of the auditorium. You begin to panic after the show. You must do something before your next platform appearance. You decide the solution is to travel around the city as quickly as you can and become acquainted with the people and their culture. This leads you to radically change your material and include stories that appeal to the people of this land. The next show comes—and you're a hit!

THE PROCESS OF DEFINING YOUR TARGET

This may sound a lot like an American Express commercial that aired a few years ago and featured Jerry Seinfeld. Don't worry, I'm not promoting him. But the commercial teaches a critical leadership lesson: we must know our target audience if we are going to communicate effectively.

Defining our target is a common teaching in church growth resources today. Dan Southerland, a church leadership expert and author of *Transitioning: Leading Your Church Through Change,* taught the importance of targeting those we want to reach in the community. The unchurched should be our target. However, we must approach targeting with the right mind-set. Southerland wrote: "Here is the balance in targeting: We should welcome and celebrate anyone who walks in our doors," and "we should also define our primary target. We must know who is in the center of our bull's-eye."[1]

Some church leaders determine a target for their church as a whole and pursue that group of people. This works well in a community where several churches are reaching different target audiences. However, it does not work well in a community where other churches are not reaching the remaining targets. After all, we are to "become all things to all [people]" (1 Cor. 9:22). How can we possibly do this as a church?

We must remember that the church is composed of groups, both ministry segments (children's ministry, youth ministry, singles ministry, etc.) and open small groups. Ministry segments and open small groups are homogeneous groups and are used to reach different target audiences.

Larry Stockstill, an expert in the area of church organization and author of *The Cell Church,* wrote about homogeneous groups in the church and how people find connections in our culture. He described how we can target those in the community through our open cell group ministries. Stockstill explained, "The word 'homogeneous' is defined by Webster's Dictionary as 'of the same or similar in nature.' Studies by noted church growth observer George Barna have shown that most Americans today find their relationships in their workplace, not in their neighborhood as in times past....Practically everyone in the cell group has a homogeneous, 'similar kind,' grouping in their life where they could gather at least four people together weekly for a 'group.'"[2]

Joel Comiskey, an authority on cell ministry and author of *Groups 12: A New Way to Mobilize Leaders and Multiply Groups in Your Church,* stated that "the new wave of cell thinking emphasizes homogeneous groups."[3] And Dale Galloway, a church growth expert and author of *The Small Group Book: The Practical Guide for Nurturing Christians and Building Churches,* wrote, "People will go where they feel drawn, not where they're assigned."[4] There is a common theme here. People in the community will go where there is a connection. This is accomplished by providing multiple connection points within the church.

Segment ministries are target ministries that reach different segments of the population. We have learned that typical segment ministries include the children's ministry, youth ministry, singles ministry, married-adult's ministry, and senior-adult's ministry. (This is not an all-inclusive list.) Each segment ministry must understand the target audiences in the population. These targets can be defined by age group, culture, marital status, occupation, interests, and many other ways. Leaders of these ministries should plan activities that appeal to the target at which they are aiming. An activity will target a group, although it may not target the intended group.

One of the main goals of every new L.I.F.E. Group (open group) in our church is to target those who are to be reached by the group. We remember what Southerland said, "We welcome everyone, but we define who is in our bull's-eye." For example, most of the people in the small group my wife and I have led are adults with children who play sports. Although this does not define everyone in the group, it is our target. What a great opportunity to reach people, especially in a community that is highly recreational with a plethora of sport leagues.

The following questions will help you define targets for your segment ministries and small groups:

1. What family groups are represented in your church's circle of influence? You can develop groups to reach all types of family groups.

2. What do the people in your area enjoy doing? You can develop groups around common recreational interests.

3. What careers are predominant in your church's circle of influence? You can develop groups by targeting employees in certain companies or from certain careers.

4. What crises are common to people in your church's circle of influence? You can develop groups to reach people who are grieving or battling with certain addictions.

Who is your church targeting? Are you taking advantage of the uniqueness of your church? The people in your church have unique qualities that connect with people in the world. A healthy church uses these gifts to reach people in its circle of influence.

THE PROCESS OF COMMUNICATING YOUR MESSAGE

Defining the target is not enough. We must also communicate our message to people in an understandable way. A lesson on communication theory is offered in the following diagram:

The Communication Process

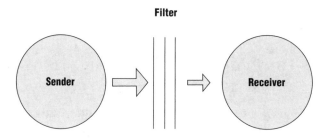

Filter

Sender → Receiver

The illustration reveals two individuals: a sender and a receiver. The message is represented by the arrows. Notice that the arrow coming from the "Sender" is larger than the arrow aiming toward the "Receiver" on the right side of the filter. The receiver filters information through his past experiences, his moral compass, and his impression of the sender.

The receiver's past experiences may include involvement with a pastor who treated him poorly, his family's religious life, or other experiences with those who claim to be Christians. The receiver's moral compass defines what he believes to be true. He may not believe that there is a God or that God is a God of love. He may believe that peace is dependent on moral living. His impressions about the sender may be based on accent, mannerisms, style of speech, or even clothes. All these filters may change the message.

Leaders must communicate effectively to penetrate these filters and clearly share their message. I am amazed at how people may twist what we say or completely block out our message. In chapter seven I shared how I made some mistakes that adversely affected the senior adults of our church. Those mistakes, which I made early in my ministry, reflected my lack of maturity to consider how leadership decisions affect groups in different ways. However, some of the senior adults began to filter everything I said through those mistakes (past experiences) and did not hear some of the good things I was communicating. They viewed me with distrust (impression), although I had not deliberately done anything against them. I was unable to communicate well with them for several months because of this failure.

THE PROCESS OF COMMUNICATING WITH YOUR COMMUNITY

The people who sit in our worship centers filter the messages our worship leaders are sending. They filter what they hear through their own preferences of style and substance. Our worship leaders must recognize this and discern how to deliver the message of truth.

As cultures change, language also changes. We can ride our holy horse and say that people should try to understand the archaic language so often used in our churches. Or we can be more concerned about the condition of their hearts and speak the truth to them with love, in a way they understand. This may take some sacrifice on our part. Changing our communication styles can cause much strife in the church. Pastors often hear the complaints of members who say, "I don't like…" (You can complete the sentence.) This message, which centers on the word *I*, is dangerous. After all, when did ministry become about us? Ministry is about what God desires.

Jesus, the greatest communicator, was concerned about the hearts of people. Just look at the parables. A great storyteller, Jesus used real-life illustrations that were part of the culture to communicate the life-changing message of love to the people. He wanted to be understood. He wanted to make a connection, and so should we.

I grew up in a church that was extremely evangelistic. Our annual revival was a highlight of the year, and our church looked forward to this important event. The purpose of the revival was to share Christ with the lost, and a guest speaker would come for a week and preach every night. We would have youth and children theme nights, which usually involved pizza or hot dogs. The speaker would share the gospel message with these groups before the service, and many would come to know Christ. This part of the night was awesome! We had a great time being with our friends and hearing the message of Christ in an interesting way.

Then we were all herded into the "Sanctuary" for the service. The evangelist would hold up a dollar bill and promise to give it to the child who behaved the best during the service. This was a gimmick that caused most of us to behave through one of the longest hours a child ever experienced. The adults loved the service, but for many children it was sheer misery.

After I became a pastor, one of the first events I planned was—you guessed it—a revival. Our first experience was incredible. Many came to know Christ, and a sense of unity began to build within the church. We had our theme nights for children, youth, men, and women, and all went well. Our church had not had an event like this for quite some time, and it was a refreshing experience. This was successful in our community, which, at that time, primarily reflected a traditional southern culture.

Our second revival did not go quite as well as the first. The community began to change quickly, as thousands of people moved into the area from the Midwest and other parts of the country. We invited a fantastic youth speaker, and many students came to know Christ on our special youth night. However, we did not experience the same success on the other theme nights, when most of the people who attended were believers.

For some reason our people no longer felt comfortable about inviting their lost friends to our revivals. We noticed that the unsaved people in attendance, especially the adults, were mostly relatives of church members. The evangelists did an excellent job of reaching this group of people. We were really excited that these family members were coming to know Christ, but we were concerned that we were not penetrating the families of non-believers in our community. They needed to be reached.

This caused our leadership team to evaluate what we were doing and determine why we were not appealing to people who were lost. We realized that we were not being relevant to our culture, and we began to dream about a creative approach to the revival week. As a result, we dropped the word *revival* and gave the week a new name, "Changing Lives One Night at a Time." We understood that the word *revival* has connotations that disturb people. For example, we didn't want people to think that they would be attending a snake-handling service. Our goal was to better communicate what we wanted to do for others—to help them experience positive change in their lives.

We featured a different speaker each night of the week, and this allowed each evangelist to focus on his strength and connect with a specific target group. Also, we invited speakers who are Christians and well known to non-believers. Brett Bulter, the famous baseball player for the Dodgers and the Braves, was our guest for a men's night event. Lisa Welchel, the actress who played "Blair" on *The Facts of Life*, was our guest for a women's night event. Those who specialize in children's ministry and youth ministry were also utilized.

The result was staggering. Our people aggressively invited their lost friends and many came to know Christ as their

Savior. We witnessed the largest number of salvations that have ever been experienced in our church in a one-week period of time. This occurred because we prayed and were responsible to communicate effectively with our target audience. "Changing Lives" week has now become one of our most important annual events.

COMMUNICATING WITH GOD THROUGH WORSHIP

Not only do we communicate with people in our communities, we who know God also communicate with Him. Have you noticed that we worship God in unique ways? If you haven't, you've been in la-la land for the past ten to fifteen years. Worship style is one of the most divisive issues in the church today.

Worship has everything to do with communication, and communication with God has everything to do with sending a heartfelt message of truth. People of different generations worship God in different ways. My parents love to sing the old hymns and prefer their use during the worship time. I grew up on contemporary Christian music and prefer to open my heart to God by singing the newer praise choruses. My parents are not wrong to worship as they do, and neither am I wrong in my style of worship.

Our hearts are wrong when we judge people because they don't worship our way. We must respect differing communication styles and be sensitive to others and how they open their hearts to God. This sensitivity comes from a heart of ministry. Our desire should be that others connect with God and we should be excited when they have opportunities to do so. This desire comes from a heart of service and our service may require our sacrifice.

The worship style my parents enjoy is great for reaching people of their culture. Contemporary styles are appropriate to use in reaching people of a contemporary culture. The challenge is to make certain that our worship styles reach the people of various target groups in our communities. We have chosen a contemporary blended approach that ministers to people of all ages. This allows participants to not only personally worship God, but to also experience the joy of being a servant as they observe others worshipping Him in their own unique way.

THE PROCESS OF COMMUNICATING YOUR PURPOSE

Does your congregation know the vision of your church? Communicating the purposes of the church is one of the most important tasks of leadership. Keeping the purposes before the people directs their focus toward pleasing God. You can successfully communicate vision and purpose to the congregation in several ways.

1. *Communicating through sermons.* The sermon is a tool the pastor uses to communicate God's message to the people. The purposes of the church should be regular themes in our sermons.

   Preaching messages on the themes of evangelism, discipleship, ministry, worship, and fellowship lays the foundation for change in the church. People want to know why change is necessary, and sermons are effective tools to teach what God expects. They are also critical for challenging ministry partners to evaluate the success of the church by God's criteria.

2. *Communicating through testimonies.* I have discovered that one of the greatest forms of communication is hearing the testimonies of those whose lives have been changed through the power of God's love. Ministry partners begin to see the importance of ministries when they hear how people have been eternally affected by those ministries.

3. *Communication through visuals.* I have been in several churches that display the five purposes on banners in

their worship center. We display our purpose statement on banners, and we have also provided a lapel
pin that has the words "Ministry Partner" around
the edge and the letters "W, B, C" in the middle. The
letters remind us that we are to "Win" (Evangelize),
"Build" (Disciple), and "Care" (Minister). The pin is
a great conversation starter. There are many other
ways to communicate the message through video and
printed materials. Be creative!

4. *Communicating through training.* I decided early in
   my ministry that I would never tell people what they
   were supposed to do without giving them a way to
   do it. This led to the development of what we call
   our "Three Steps to Maturity" classes. These training
   classes are foundation classes for our ministry partners; they learn how to evangelize, become disciples,
   and minister to those in need. They learn how to do
   what God has called us to do. We use the strategy
   plan of the church to help participants understand
   the process of moving people closer to God. We
   must train our people to be involved in this process
   if it is to become a reality.

THE PROCESS OF COMMUNICATING ACCOUNTABILITY

Communication is also important in the process of holding
church leadership accountable for their tasks. Leaders must
know what is being accomplished in the church because this is
critical for proper evaluation. The strategy map is a great communication tool that the leadership team uses as a scoreboard
to reveal the strengths and weaknesses of ministry.

Soon after our leadership team began using the strategy
map, I asked our ministerial staff to map the people in their
area of ministry. One of my staff ministers came and told me
what it revealed. The map showed that they were generating
many new friends through their ministry. However, they were

not properly following up on those who had made connection to the church. The map showed that the ministry was out of balance. Corrections were made and this quickly resulted in more people coming to know Christ. For more information on mapping the results of ministry, look at the section entitled "Measuring Success" in chapter five.

Leaders must hold their team accountable for their tasks. This requires regular times for communicating with team members to ensure that ministry is being performed. The accountability process will vary depending on the leadership structure of your church.

How well are you communicating? The healthy church delivers the messages that need to be heard in ways that are understandable and motivating. How motivating is your message?

9

THE PARTNERSHIP

Two are better than one, because they have a good return for their work: If one falls down, his friend can help him up. But pity the man who falls and has no one to help him up! Also, if two lie down together, they will keep warm. But how can one keep warm alone? Though one may be overpowered, two can defend themselves. A cord of three strands is not quickly broken.

—ECCLESIASTES 4:9–12

Mastering Team Leadership

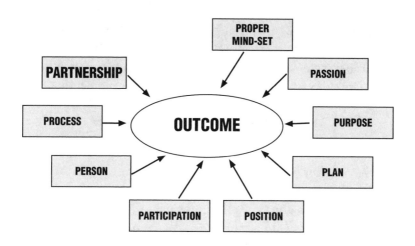

Baseball season is here again. You can't believe how quickly the years seem to zoom by as you grow older. Baseball season is one of the busiest times of the year as you hurriedly try to leave work and deliver your son to what seems like daily practices.

This will be a different type of baseball season for you. You've been asked by the commissioner of the league to coach one of the teams. A few years ago you served as an assistant coach and enjoyed your experience, but you have declined recent invitations because of a hectic work and family schedule.

Practices begin and things seem to be going well. The team is composed of some really talented players and you are excited about the possibilities. You're already dreaming about receiving the championship trophy as a rookie manager. The first game comes and, to your great surprise, the team is blown out; losing 9 to 1. You think this is just a fluke and are certain that things will get better in the second game. Unfortunately, this is not the case. The final score of game two: 11 to 2.

You can't believe it. How in the world can a team with such talented players be playing so poorly? The answer to that question is obvious to those on the outside. The players aren't playing as a team; they are playing as individuals. Your wife points out that the players are more interested in receiving glory for their personal play than helping the other team members become successful. The time has come for a team meeting.

A Theological Foundation
for Cooperation

Have you ever been on a team like this? Maybe it was an athletic team or a team in the workplace. The organizations with the best players don't always win the game. The teams consisting of members who appreciate and help one another have a much better opportunity to accomplish great things. The ability of people to work as a team has a direct bearing on the outcome of ministries performed in the church.

The church is here to accomplish great things. The healthy

church has a group of leaders who work together as a team to ensure organizational success. Our success is dependent upon how well we work to develop fully devoted followers of Christ.

The Bible gives instruction on the importance of teamwork. God teaches us that we are to work together for the kingdom of God. The following truths lay a theological foundation for cooperating with one another.

Truth #1: We are gifted differently.

Read again the words of the apostle Paul. He wrote: "It was he who gave some to be apostles, some to be prophets, some to be evangelists, and some to be pastors and teachers, to prepare God's people for works of service, so that the body of Christ may be built up until we all reach unity in the faith and in the knowledge of the Son of God and become mature, attaining to the whole measure of the fullness of Christ" (Eph. 4:11–13). Theologian Arthur W. Pink taught that believers are to function as the body of Christ. He wrote: "Christ has a natural body, by virtue of His incarnation. He has a sacramental body, which is seen in the Lord's Supper. He has a ministerial body, the local church or assembly, where His ordinances are administered and His truth proclaimed."[1] Members of this body must work together to ensure that God's truth is proclaimed.

Truth #2: We become the body of Christ when we work together.

Paul taught that we are the body of Christ and that each of us is important. He wrote, "Now you are the body of Christ, and each one of you is a part of it" (1 Cor. 12:27). He said that we are to rely on one another as we function as one body—the body of Christ.

Truth #3: We are to perform ministry in groups.

Jesus sent His followers into the world to conduct ministry in groups. Luke showed this when he wrote, "After this the Lord appointed seventy-two others and sent them two by two ahead of him to every town and place where he was about to go" (Luke 10:1). We also read that a group of servants were selected to meet the needs of people in the church in the Book of Acts.

> Brothers, choose seven men from among you who are known to be full of the Spirit and wisdom. We will turn this responsibility over to them and will give our attention to prayer and the ministry of the word." This proposal pleased the whole group. They chose Stephen, a man full of faith and of the Holy Spirit; also Philip, Procorus, Nicanor, Timon, Parmenas, and Nicolas from Antioch, a convert to Judaism. They presented these men to the apostles, who prayed and laid their hands on them.
>
> —ACTS 6:3–6

Truth #4: We honor one another through our devotion to one another.

Paul communicated this truth when he wrote:

> Love must be sincere. Hate what is evil; cling to what is good. Be devoted to one another in brotherly love. Honor one another above yourselves. Never be lacking in zeal, but keep your spiritual fervor, serving the Lord. Be joyful in hope, patient in affliction, faithful in prayer. Share with God's people who are in need. Practice hospitality.
>
> —ROMANS 12:9–13

Truth #5: We are to be considerate of one another.

Dale Moody, theologian and author, taught on the subject of consideration and how it reveals God's love. He wrote: "The participle translated love is philostorgos, a combination of storge and philia, of mother love and brother love. Preference for one another implies a feeling of consideration."[2] Paul emphasized the importance of consideration when he wrote: "Do nothing out of selfish ambition or vain conceit, but in humility consider others better than yourselves. Each of you should look not only to your own interests, but also to the interests of others" (Phil. 2:3–4).

Truth #6: Two are better than one.

The book of Ecclesiastes teaches us why two are better than one. The scripture states:

> Two are better than one, because they have a good return for their work: If one falls down, his friend can help him up. But pity the man who falls and has no one to help him up! Also, if two lie down together, they will keep warm. But how can one keep warm alone? Though one may be overpowered, two can defend themselves. A cord of three strands is not quickly broken.
>
> —Ecclesiastes 4:9–12

Synergism

When two or more people work together as a team, they produce what is known as "synergism." The presence of synergism differentiates a team from a group. Pat MacMillan wrote:

> This primary difference between a team and any other type of group is synergism. Many groups have a common purpose; most even see some level of cooperation. But in a true team the combination of factors and the intensity and consistency with which they are applied allows a team to experience results on a regular basis.[3]

He added that "teamwork is cooperation at its highest level, and the level of cooperation drives the level of the results."[4]

The results vary, depending on the level of cooperation. When a group becomes a true team, the results of its work are greater than the added results of separate group members. For example, I go out and share Jesus with my friends and win three people to Christ. You go out and share Jesus with your friends and win three people to Christ. The result is that six people come to know Christ. This is great.

However, synergy happens when we work together and the results go beyond these "added" results. For example, you and I join together and plan an intentionally evangelistic event to reach the residents in our neighborhood. We work together as a team and invite 100 families to come and hear one of your friends (a professional athlete) share his testimony. The result is that forty people accept Christ as their Savior. That's synergism. Teamwork multiplied the results.

A healthy church will have leaders who work together in a way that produces "multiplied" results, not just "added" results. The healthy church uses a combination strategy where people share Christ one-on-one and people work together to plan events where large numbers can hear the good news.

FUNCTIONING AS A CREW

Theresa Kline wrote about teams in her book entitled *Remaking Teams: The Revolutionary Research-Based Guide That Puts Theory into Practice.* She wrote:

> Unfortunately, there is as yet no common way to talk about different types of teams. This situation, however, is changing. In the latter part of the 1990s there has been a concerted effort on the part of several researchers to tackle the task of building a taxonomy of teams. Their work suggests that there are fundamental differences between team types and that it is important to attend to them. This line of research has revealed several common threads in what differentiates team types, including degree of structure of the task, prescriptiveness of the roles of the members, nature of the communication between members, nature of the information exchange between members, and type and degree of sharing of common goals among the members. Depending on where the team falls on these dimensions, there are ramifications for where effort needs to be placed to make the team more effective.[6]

She introduced a specific type of team—she called it a crew—that correlates well with the leadership team in the church. The crew is a well-defined team that moves in a unified direction when the following conditions are met:

1. The task is highly structured.
2. Roles are highly prescribed.
3. Communication links are well defined.
4. Need for information exchange is high.
5. Common, short-term goals are shared.[7]

The crew must row in the same direction to achieve success. This is illustrated in MacMillan's book, *The Performance Factor: Unlocking the Secrets of Teamwork*. He used the picture of a boat containing crewmembers who were identified by arrows.

The Crew Aligned With Purpose

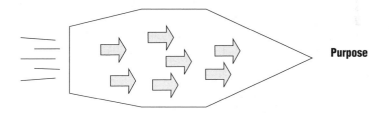

The diagram above reveals that the crew is working together toward a common purpose. However, problems arise on the team when its members begin rowing away from the team's purpose. The following diagram shows that the crew is in trouble:

The Crew Misaligned With Team Purpose

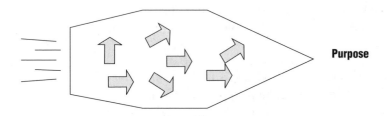

Three crew members are rowing toward the team purpose, and four crew members are rowing in alternate directions. Which crew member do you think causes the team the most difficulty? Some may think it is the crew member who is rowing in a direction farthest away from the team's purpose. Actually, this is the easiest problem to correct. His direction away from the team purpose is so obvious that the other crew members can just kick him off the boat (please don't forget the life jacket). The crew members who are rowing slightly off course can cause the most difficulty because they are hard to detect. They cause just enough friction to cause the team to miss its destination.

MacMillan's Characteristics of a High Performance Team

MacMillan shared six characteristics of teams who achieve synergism. They are illustrated using the following diagram:

The Characteristics of a Highly Effective Team

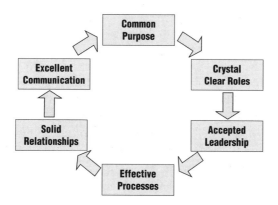

1. *Common Purpose.* According to MacMillan, "The
    single most important ingredient in team success
    is a clear, common, compelling purpose."[11] Randy
    Frazee emphasized the importance that purpose
    plays in developing a biblical community in his
    book entitled *The Connecting Church: Beyond Small
    Groups to Authentic Community.* He wrote that
    "biblical community is a collection of people who
    gather around a common biblical purpose and
    common principles."[12] We discussed the purposes
    of the church in chapter three.

    Accomplishing the purposes becomes our reason
    to work together as a team. They are at the heart of
    our existence. One of my football heroes, Bear Bry-
    ant, talked about the importance of having the same
    passion when he said, "I'm just a simple plow hand
    from Arkansas, but I have learned over the years
    how to hold a team together. How to lift some men
    up, how to calm others down, until finally they've
    got one heartbeat, together, a team."[13] A team that
    operates with one heartbeat is powerful and effective.

    Gene Mims defined a clear purpose for the
    kingdom-focused church when he wrote that the

church "exists to transform unbelievers into Christ-like believers and to mature these believers into kingdom multipliers of the message of Christ."[14] The healthy church has leaders who work together to make certain that this becomes a reality.

2. *Crystal Clear Roles.* MacMillan wrote: "High performance teams are characterized by crystal clear roles. Every team member is clear about his or her particular role, as well as those of the other team members. Roles are about how we design, divide, and deploy the work of the team."[15]

   He also taught that five qualities are valuable in designing roles for team members; emphasizing that the roles must be "clear, complete, compatible, complementary, and consensual."[16] Roles that do not include these design elements can cause friction between team members and work against team unity and synergism. We examined leadership roles and relay team ministry in chapter six. A successful relay team ministry has leaders who clearly understand their responsibilities and are capable to fulfill their roles.

3. *Accepted Leadership.* According to MacMillan, "high performance teams need clear, competent leadership. When such leadership is lacking, groups lose their way."[17] He defined the roles of a team leader, stating that they are to be direction setters, boundary managers, facilitators, negotiators, and coaches.[18] Teams that experience synergism have leaders who fulfill these roles. In chapter seven we learned about factors that influence the development of qualities that enable church leaders to be successful. Leaders must be able to use multiple leadership styles, understand their personal styles, master four fundamental capabilities, and give evidence of specific leadership traits.

4. *Effective Processes.* MacMillan wrote, "Teams and processes go together. The playbook of a football team or the score sheet of a string quartet clearly outlines their processes."[19] A team can use the processes it follows to measure results and evaluate if synergism is taking place. The leader must use this information to hold team members accountable for their duties. The strategy of church ministry described in chapter four is a process of ministry that becomes the playbook for the church. Leaders can use this to determine necessary actions that accomplish the purposes of the church.

5. *Solid Relationships.* Relationships can bring unity or cause division on the team. Team members do not necessarily need the same interests to remain unified. The team is actually strengthened through diversity. MacMillan taught:
   "The diversity of skill, experience, and knowledge needed effectively and creatively to divide the task almost preclude high levels of friendship, which is most often based on common interests.... The more different a team is, the smarter it can be. A team whose members look at the world through the different lenses of function, gender, ethnicity, personality, experience, and perspective has a decided advantage over a more homogenous group."[20]

6. *Excellent Communication.* Cooperation within the group requires clear communication between team members. MacMillan wrote, "Communication is the very means of cooperation.... A team, or the organization in which it resides, cannot move faster than it communicates."[21] The process of communication is the theme of chapter eight. We learned that success occurs when we effectively communicate with God, with those in the organization, and with those in our community.

EVALUATING YOUR TEAM

Is your team producing synergistic results? If it is not, you will find it helpful to answer the following questions:

- Do team members understand what the team is to accomplish?

- What is your team attempting to accomplish?

- Do team members know the importance of fulfilling their roles?

- What roles do people play on your team?

- Is the leader of the team accepted by team members?

- Are you accepted as a team leader? Why or why not?

- Do team members understand the importance of the plan developed by the team?

- Do you have a plan to accomplish the team's purpose?

- Are relationships between team members causing a sense of unity or division?

- Who is causing division on your team? Why?

- How well does the team communicate?

- Is your team communicating its purpose, roles, expectations, and plan, as well as the personal needs of its members?

AVOIDING THE FIVE DYSFUNCTIONS

Leadership expert Patrick Lencioni has identified five dysfunctions that cause teams to fail. The church team must be aware of these dysfunctions and avoid them if it is to succeed and experience the results that God desires. The five dysfunctions are illustrated in the diagram below.[22]

The Five Dysfunctions Pyramid

Level One—Absence of Trust

Lencioni wrote that this dysfunction stems from "an unwillingness to be vulnerable within the group. Team members who are not genuinely open with one another about their mistakes and weaknesses make it impossible to build a foundation of trust."[23] Trust is the foundation on which teams are built. If trust does not exist, there will be no success. This has been a very important part of our team culture. Team members must know that each person cares about everyone on the team. They must also trust people on the team to react in godly ways when difficulties arise. Distrust is one of the strongest weapons Satan uses against teamwork in the church.

Level Two—Fear of Conflict

Lencioni taught that "teams that lack trust are incapable of engaging in unfiltered and passionate debate of ideas."[24] Conflict is positive because of the difference of ideas. Conflict is negative when it becomes personal and is used to tear others down. Early in my ministry, I interpreted disagreement with my ideas about ministry as a personal attack. This caused an unhealthy culture in our teams, and people were reluctant to share opposing ideas. Unfortunately this caused us to miss wonderful ministry opportunities. It also revealed my self-centeredness and weakness as a leader. I'm happy to say that I have experienced much improvement in this area, and it has resulted in much better communication and the exchange of great ideas.

Level Three—Lack of Commitment

Lencioni noted that team members who do not "air their opinions in the course of passionate and open debate . . . rarely, if ever, buy in and commit to decisions."[25] Participants must buy in to the purpose and plan of the team if success is to be realized. I have found that this is true on our team. Those who share ideas and are appreciated for sharing them are willing to commit to ministry activities. They know that their opinion is valued.

Level Four—Avoidance of Accountability

Lencioni wrote: "Without committing to a clear plan of action, even the most focused and driven people often hesitate to call their peers on actions and behaviors that seem counterproductive to the good of the team."[26] Team members must be willing to be held accountable and to hold others accountable. This occurs when they are passionate about accomplishing a common goal. I have learned that clear expectations are necessary, and that results must be measured in a clear way.

Level Five—Inattention to Results

Lencioni explained that this dysfunction occurs "when team members put their individual needs . . . above the collective goals of the team."[27] The selfish condition of the heart causes unwillingness to do whatever it takes to obtain the desired results. A frequent statement at our church is that we want "God-sized results." We don't want results that can be explained by man's ability alone. For this to happen, people on the team must be fully devoted to God, and they must desire to please Him through their work. The focus must be on what He expects from us.

Are you a team or are you a group of individuals who only care about self? Teams that produce God-sized results function as a body and not as individual parts. The time has come to decide as a team to accomplish results that can come only through God's power and our working together as His body.

10

THE PROGRAM

Commit to the LORD whatever you do, and your plans will succeed.

—PROVERBS 16:3

Developing a Recipe for Success

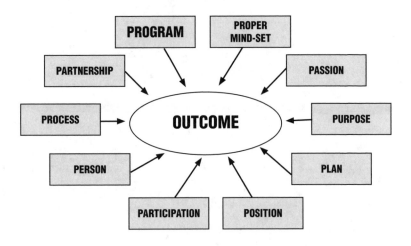

The church frequently uses the word *program* to describe ministry activities. For example, we speak of the Sunday school program, or the Discipleship Training program. I think of computers when I hear the word *program*. A computer program consists of a combination of action commands that its creator has developed to produce a particular result. This relates well to the ministry of the church. The church program is not a single ministry action, but a combination of ministry activities that, in a healthy church, accomplish God's purposes. The purpose of this chapter is to follow the recipe of ministry actions in this book to develop a healthy church.

A RECIPE FOR SUCCESS

What does the following recipe produce?

    2 slices bacon, diced
    1 tbsp. unsalted butter
    1 medium onion, cut into ½ inch pieces
    1 bay leaf
    ½ tbsp. chopped fresh thyme
    1 cup water
    1 can clams (6 ½ ounces)
    3 red or white new potatoes, cut into ½ inch pieces
    1 cup heavy cream
    ground black pepper
    1 tbsp. chopped fresh parsley[1]

This is a recipe for one of my favorite foods—clam chowder. I don't cook very much, as my wife can attest. However, one day several years ago we were bored, and I decided to try my hand in the kitchen. My wife is an incredible cook and I knew that she would be of great help to me. I relied on her expertise to assist me as I prepared my very first batch of chowder. This was an awesome experience. We had fun talking and laughing as we worked diligently and anticipated a tasty treat. Although we had begun with the purpose of cooking a particular dish, the process along the way was very rewarding. The outcome was a stronger relationship and, of course, a full stomach.

Our journey through this book has been a process of learning the ingredients for a healthy church. We are seeking to have a healthy church, and we desire that relationships will be strengthened along the way. The time has now come for us to evaluate our church and begin putting the ingredients together. Remember, the blueprint is used to construct a ministry plan for the church and as a diagnostic tool to discover areas of sickness that need to be addressed. Follow the recipe steps by completing the exercises that appear below.

Step One: Begin with the proper mind-set.

We learned in chapter one that we must measure the success of the church in the right way. The healthy church is the body of Christ and functions as Christ's body. To accomplish this, we must serve God by serving others. We learned that not all people in the church will have a ministry. Some are new believers and are growing toward servanthood. One rule of thumb is to divide the participants into thirds. One third should be seekers, another third should be growing into servanthood, and the final third should be serving. The makeup of the church is the result of our efforts in ministry. If we exert equal effort in the areas of evangelism, discipleship, and ministry, this should be reflected in the results.

Let's think of this in another way. Seekers, in theory, are not members of the church. If we take them out of the equation, we can divide the membership of the church into halves. One half of the members should be serving, and the other half should be growing into servanthood. Use the following scale to grade your church. Remember, this is not scientific. The culture of your community and the dynamics of your church may alter these results.

Grade A = 50 percent involvement of members in ministry.
Grade B = 40–50 percent involvement of members in ministry.
Grade C = 30–40 percent involvement of members in ministry.

Grade D = 20–30 percent involvement of members in ministry.

Grade F = Less than 20 percent involvement of members in ministry.

Step Two: Operate out of the correct passion.

The correct passion is a passion for God. The ministries of the church should exist to fulfill the commands to love the Lord our God with all of our heart, soul, mind, and strength and to reveal this love by serving others. The incorrect passion is to perform ministry according to the traditions of men. Man's theology is worldly and produces activities for the purpose of human advancement. We learned in chapter two that we are to begin with the needs of people, not the existing ministries, when we develop the ministry strategy of the church.

It is important that we evaluate the ministry activities of the church and discern if they are performed because of passion for God or passion for self. List all the ministries of your church in the space below and place a check under the passion that best describes them.

The Theology Behind Current Ministries

Ministry Description	Passion for God	Passion for Self

Step Three: Understand your purpose.

What is your purpose? Does your church have a statement that defines its mission? We learned in chapter three that a purpose statement should be clear, compelling, and measurable. It should also direct the church to accomplish the purposes of worship, fellowship, evangelism, discipleship, and ministry. You may want to enlist some key leaders to help you develop a purpose statement that is unique to your church. Write it in the space below.

_____

_____

_____

_____

_____

_____

_____

Step Four: Create a plan to accomplish the results God desires.

We learned a ministry strategy that incorporates the five purposes of the church and ensures that they are being fulfilled. Our task in the process is to lead the seeker to be saved and the saved to become servants. People are located at one of five identification points, and we perform different activities to reach them. Use the Strategy Map below to evaluate your current ministries and discover areas of need by following the instructions that follow the diagram. Once again, you may want to enlist some key leaders to help you.

Strategy Map

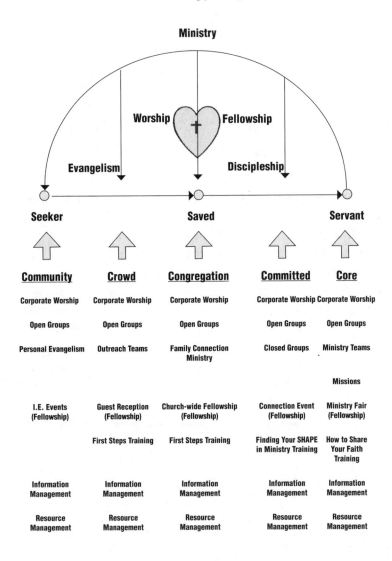

Circle ministry areas that need to be developed or improved, and give them dedicated attention. For example, you may circle Intentionally Evangelistic Events (I.E. Events), which can be critical to your success in reaching the unchurched. List ideas for events, and encourage your members to invite others to attend them. You may also circle "How to Share Your Faith Training." This is vital to help believers cultivate relationships with the lost. An Intentionally Evangelistic Event is of no use when members do not have relationships with people who need God. They will have no one to invite to the event, and it will become a church-family fellowship instead of an event to share the good news with seekers.

Pray diligently about the ministries God wants your church to perform. It should be our desire to experience God-sized results, and this will not happen if we develop plans without the inspiration of God. We need to hear from God and understand His plan for our churches. God wants us to develop servants. The goal is to have a well-balanced plan that assists the church in leading people to become involved in ministry. Pray for God's wisdom concerning new ministries and also for members who will serve in them. Use the strategy map to share your ministry vision with the congregation, and identify areas of need. Ask your members to seek God's direction concerning their involvement.

Step Five: Discover the spiritual position of others.

Healthy churches know who they are reaching through their ministries, and keeping information about this is critical. Complete the following People Map by identifying people who are in ministry partners' circles of influence, current church "friends" (prospects), and ministry partners (members). List the names of people who are currently located under each location point. If you need to review how to map the people, review the section "The Journey" in chapter five.

The People Map

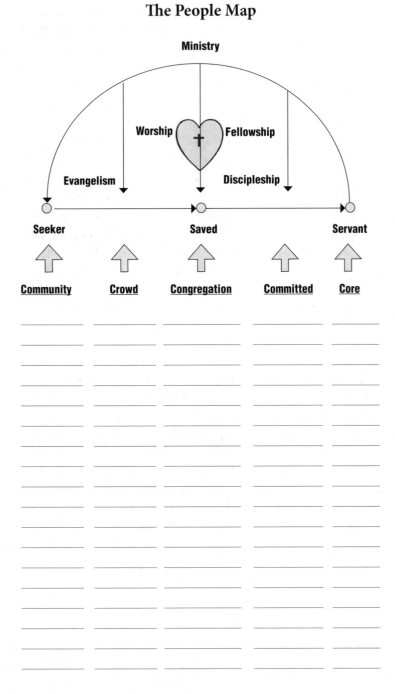

Step Six: Lead people to participate according to their giftedness.

In chapter six, we learned how the healthy church assigns leaders according to its purpose and ministry strategy. Each church needs a Mission Control Team to develop a purpose statement and assist in the operation and evaluation of its ministries.

The diagram entitled Leadership Team Strategy Map reveals that the evangelism leader is responsible for the ministries that help lead the seeker to be saved. The discipleship leader is responsible for the ministries that encourage and guide the saved to be servants. The ministry leader is responsible for involving people in ministry teams that accomplish the ministry of the church. The worship leader is responsible to lead people to connect their hearts with God's heart. The fellowship leader is responsible to help people connect with each other.

Ministry teams serve in each area of ministry in the church. For example, intentionally evangelistic events are conducted by an Intentionally Evangelistic Event Team, which is led by an Intentionally Evangelistic Event Team Leader. The leaders of ministry teams are accountable to the church leader over them (evangelism leader or discipleship leader).

Look again at the Leadership Team Strategy Map and answer the following questions.

Mission Control Team

- Who is your evangelism leader?

- Who is your discipleship leader?

- Who is your ministry leader?

- Who is your worship leader?

- Who is your fellowship leader?

Leadership Team Strategy Map

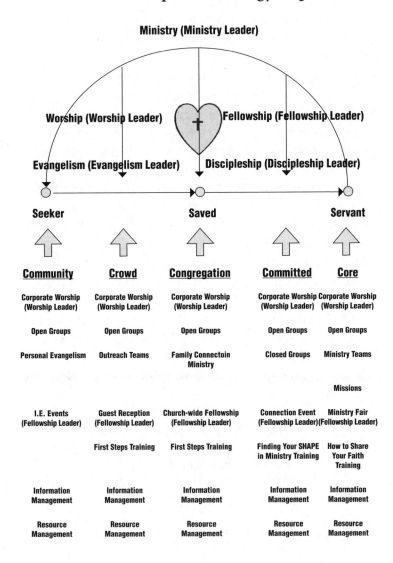

Ministry (Ministry Leader)

Worship (Worship Leader) Fellowship (Fellowship Leader)

Evangelism (Evangelism Leader) Discipleship (Discipleship Leader)

Seeker Saved Servant

Community	Crowd	Congregation	Committed	Core
Corporate Worship (Worship Leader)	Corporate Worship (Worship Leader)	Corporate Worship (Worship Leader)	Corporate Worship (Worship Leader)	Corporate Worship (Worship Leader)
Open Groups	Open Groups	Open Groups	Open Groups	Open Groups
Personal Evangelism	Outreach Teams	Family Connectoin Ministry	Closed Groups	Ministry Teams
				Missions
I.E. Events (Fellowship Leader)	Guest Reception (Fellowship Leader)	Church-wide Fellowship (Fellowship Leader)	Connection Event (Fellowship Leader)	Ministry Fair (Fellowship Leader)
	First Steps Training	First Steps Training	Finding Your SHAPE in Ministry Training	How to Share Your Faith Training
Information Management	Information Management	Information Management	Information Management	Information Management
Resource Management	Resource Management	Resource Management	Resource Management	Resource Management

Other Key Leaders:

- Who is your Open Small Group Leader(s)?

- Who is your Closed Group Leader(s)?

- Who is your Outreach Team Leader(s)?

- Who teaches your "First Steps" Training class(es)?

- Who teaches your "How to Share Your Faith" training class(es)?

- Who teaches your "Finding Your SHAPE in Ministry" training class(es)?

- Who oversees information management?

- Who oversees your management of resources?

- Who is your Family Connection Leader(s)? (Deacon Ministry)

Your name may follow many of these questions if you are a minister in a small church. However, the more responsibilities you have, the less effective you are. You must work to develop a team of leaders who can assist you in ministry. This becomes easier as the church begins to grow and you train members to minister to others. Evangelism is the beginning point, and you must make it a priority if the church is to grow. You must be careful to select leaders who have spiritual gifts appropriate for their task and are also able to use various leadership styles as the situation demands. You must know the leadership strengths of your team so you can take advantage of them.

Step Seven: Encourage participants to be the leaders that God desires.

Leaders will make you or break you. A great plan led by great leaders succeeds, but a great plan led by weak leaders fails. The ability of leaders to influence correctly will have a direct effect on the results of your church ministry. Spend time with your leaders and assess their spiritual gifts, leadership strengths, and personal styles. All your leaders should take the "Finding Your SHAPE in Ministry" class or a similar spiritual gifts class to determine their spiritual gifts.

Chapter seven identified six leadership styles: the visionary, coercive, affiliative, democratic, pacesetting, and coaching styles. It also defined four personal styles: dominance, interaction, steadiness, and cautiousness. Consider your mission control leaders and the top two strengths of each in the areas of spiritual giftedness, predominant leadership styles, and personal styles. Record your conclusions in the space below.

Evangelism Leader

Spiritual Gifts:

1. _____
2. _____

Predominant Leadership Styles:

1. _____
2. _____

Personal Styles:

_____

_____

Discipleship Leader

Spiritual Gifts:

1. _____
2. _____

Predominant Leadership Styles:

1. _____
2. _____

Personal Styles:

_____

_____

Ministry Leader
Spiritual Gifts:
1. _____
2. _____

Predominant Leadership Styles:
1. _____
2. _____

Personal Styles:

_____

_____

Worship Leader
Spiritual Gifts:
1. _____
2. _____

Predominant Leadership Styles:
1. _____
2. _____

Personal Styles:

_____

_____

Fellowship Leader
Spiritual Gifts:
1. _____
2. _____

Predominant Leadership Styles:
1. _____
2. _____

Personal Styles:

_____

_____

We also learned that leaders should have certain leadership traits. Prospective leaders should be prayerfully evaluated by these traits before they are asked to serve in ministry. (See Exodus 18:17–23.) As you seek God's direction, I believe that He will reveal to you if an individual is a proper fit for ministry in a given leadership role. Church leaders should use the same process for those under their leadership. For example, the evangelism leader will want to learn more about the spiritual gifts and leadership styles of the open small group leader(s) involved in evangelism, the personal evangelism leader, the intentionally evangelistic event leader, and the outreach teams leader.

Step Eight: Communicate effectively during the process.

Chapter eight emphasized the process of communication. The leaders of a healthy church have a vital role in effectively communicating the good news of Christ to the community, worship to God, and a plan of accountability to those who serve.

Communicating with the culture—Using statistical information from the census or other relevant information, answer the following questions about those who live in the ministry radius of your church:

- What is the population?

- What is the socioeconomic makeup?

- What are the predominant family unit types?

- How many children live in this area?

- How many youth live in this area?

- How many young adults live in this area?

- How many middle aged-adults live in this area?

- How many senior adults live in this area?

- How many single adults live in this area?

- How many different ethnic groups live in this area?

- What types of jobs are predominant in this area?

- What do people do for recreation?

- How many schools are in this area?

The answers to these questions will help you know your target audience. This is the key to successfully plan events that appeal to people in your community and present the message of truth in an understandable way.

Communicating with God through worship—We worship God in different ways. Make certain that your worship actually connects you with God. Assess your worship style to ensure that its elements are relevant and have meaning to people of different cultures and generations. Build a culture of sacrifice in which people sacrifice their worship preferences for the good of others. This is actually an act of worship that connects us with the heart of God. Worship is not about what I want; it is about what God wants from me. He wants my obedience, sacrifice, and praise. These bring glory to God.

Answer the following questions:

- Are we connecting with God?

- Are we communicating with God through worship styles that reach people in our community?

- Are we making sacrifices so others can connect with God?

Communicating accountability—The Ministry Strategy Activity Map, the People Map, and the Leadership Team Strategy Map are communication tools for the accountability process. The Ministry Strategy Activity Map identifies the activities of the church and is a road map for the leadership team to use as it plans. The People Map reveals if there is balance in ministry and if the church is effective in leading people to become servants. The Leadership Team Strategy Map shows any vacancies that must be filled in the leadership structure. When these three tools are used in evaluation meetings, they help leaders to determine areas of strength and weakness in the church.

Step Nine: Partner together as a team.

Pat MacMillan's book *The Performance Factor: Unlocking the Secrets of Teamwork* defines highly effective teams by six characteristics. They know their purpose, they understand their roles, they accept their leaders, they use effective processes, they have solid relationships, and they have excellent communication.

Answer the following questions to help you develop a strategy for team success:

- How will you keep your purpose before your team?

- How will you assign clear roles to all your team members?

- What will you do to become accepted as a leader?

- What processes will you use to hold your team members accountable?

- How will you build relationships between team members?

- What will you do to ensure that proper communication exists between your team members?

Step Ten: Combine the ingredients.

The recipe is written. Now the ministry must be performed. A strategy is only effective if the people who develop it follow through and complete the activities that have been planned. A healthy church not only has a plan; in addition, its leaders work the plan and make adjustments when it is not working. The health of your church depends on your steps of hearing from God and fulfilling His call.

God's call for us to conduct his ministry is worth our sacrifice. Are you willing? Are you listening? Are you planning? Are you serving?

Appendix A
THE SPIRITUAL ASSESSMENT

Instructions: Answer the following questions on a scale of 0 to 10, with 0 meaning never true and 10 meaning always true.

A. Loving (Worship and Fellowship)

1. I truly worship God when I attend a corporate worship service.

   Exalt the LORD our God and worship at his holy mountain, for the LORD our God is holy.
   —PSALM 99:9

   0   1   2   3   4   5   6   7   8   9   10

2. I have close companionship with God.

   A man of many companions may come to ruin, but there is a friend who sticks closer than a brother.
   —PROVERBS 18:24

   0   1   2   3   4   5   6   7   8   9   10

3. I spend time alone with God on a daily basis.

   In the morning, O LORD, you hear my voice; in the morning I lay my requests before you and wait in expectation.
   —PSALM 5:3

   0   1   2   3   4   5   6   7   8   9   10

4. I regularly make sacrifices to please God.

   Greater love has no one than this, that he lay down his life for his friends.

   —JOHN 15:13

   0   1   2   3   4   5   6   7   8   9   10

5. I regularly put the needs of others before my own needs.

   Just as the Son of Man did not come to be served, but to serve, and to give his life as a ransom for many.

   —MATTHEW 20:28

   0   1   2   3   4   5   6   7   8   9   10

6. I am patient.

   Love is patient.

   —1 CORINTHIANS 13:4

   0   1   2   3   4   5   6   7   8   9   10

7. I am kind.

   Love is kind.

   —1 CORINTHIANS 13:4

   0   1   2   3   4   5   6   7   8   9   10

8. I protect God's reputation.

   Love does not delight in evil but rejoices with the truth. It always protects.

   —1 CORINTHIANS 13:6–7

   0   1   2   3   4   5   6   7   8   9   10

9. I protect the reputations of others.

Because Joseph her husband was a righteous man and did not want to expose her to public disgrace.
—MATTHEW 1:19

0   1   2   3   4   5   6   7   8   9   10

10. I am humble.

Love…does not boast.
—1 CORINTHIANS 13:4

0   1   2   3   4   5   6   7   8   9   10

B. Winning (Evangelism)

1. I have identified the lost who live in my circle of influence.

For the Son of Man came to seek and to save what was lost.
—LUKE 19:10

0   1   2   3   4   5   6   7   8   9   10

2. I pray daily for the lost who live in my circle of influence.

My prayer is not for them alone. I pray also for those who will believe in me through their message.
—JOHN 17:20

0   1   2   3   4   5   6   7   8   9   10

3. I share my faith with others daily.

For we cannot help speaking about what we have seen and heard.
—ACTS 4:20

0   1   2   3   4   5   6   7   8   9   10

4. I use my spiritual gifts to serve others and build relationships with the lost.

It was he who gave some to be apostles, some to be prophets, some to be evangelists, and some to be pastors and teachers, to prepare God's people for works of service.

—EPHESIANS 4:11–12

0   1   2   3   4   5   6   7   8   9   10

5. I invite those in my circle of influence to come to intentionally evangelistic events.

Go to the street corners and invite to the banquet anyone you find.

—MATTHEW 22:9

0   1   2   3   4   5   6   7   8   9   10

6. I allow God to use me as a witness by living a life that is free of sin.

Finally, brothers, whatever is true, whatever is noble, whatever is right, whatever is pure, whatever is lovely, whatever is admirable—if anything is excellent or praiseworthy—think about such things.

—PHILIPPIANS 4:8

0   1   2   3   4   5   6   7   8   9   10

7. My words and actions are consistent.

About Jesus of Nazareth," they replied. "He was a prophet, powerful in word and deed before God and all the people.

—LUKE 24:20

0   1   2   3   4   5   6   7   8   9   10

8. I live a life of joy.

   But the fruit of the Spirit is...joy.

   —GALATIANS 5:22

   0 1 2 3 4 5 6 7 8 9 10

9. I have a burden for those who do not know Christ.

   When he saw the crowds, he had compassion on them, because they were harassed and helpless, like sheep without a shepherd.

   —MATTHEW 9:36

   0 1 2 3 4 5 6 7 8 9 10

10. I am willing to put myself at risk to share the good news of Christ with those who are lost.

    For even the Son of Man did not come to be served, but to serve, and to give his life as a ransom for many.

    —MARK 10:45

    0 1 2 3 4 5 6 7 8 9 10

C. Building (Discipleship)

1. I live a life of self-control.

   But the fruit of the Spirit is...self-control.

   —GALATIANS 5:22–23

   0 1 2 3 4 5 6 7 8 9 10

2. I am at peace with God.

   But the fruit of the Spirit is...peace.

   —GALATIANS 5:22

   0 1 2 3 4 5 6 7 8 9 10

3. I trust God in every situation.

Do not let your hearts be troubled. Trust in God; trust also in me.

—JOHN 14:1

0   1   2   3   4   5   6   7   8   9   10

4. I daily practice the discipline of prayer.

And pray in the Spirit on all occasions with all kinds of prayers and requests. With this in mind, be alert and always keep on praying for all the saints.

—EPHESIANS 6:18

0   1   2   3   4   5   6   7   8   9   10

5. I daily practice the discipline of Bible study.

Your word is a lamp to my feet and a light for my path.

—PSALM 119:105

0   1   2   3   4   5   6   7   8   9   10

6. I attend a group meeting with believers who hold me accountable to live obediently.

Every day they continued to meet together in the temple courts. They broke bread in their homes and ate together with glad and sincere hearts.

—ACTS 2:46

0   1   2   3   4   5   6   7   8   9   10

7. I participate in corporate worship to God weekly.

You Samaritans worship what you do not know; we worship what we do know, for salvation is from the Jews.

—JOHN 4:22

0   1   2   3   4   5   6   7   8   9   10

8. I memorize God's Word weekly.

I have hidden your word in my heart that I might not sin against you.

—PSALM 119:11

0   1   2   3   4   5   6   7   8   9   10

9. I am regularly mentored by another believer.

Don't let anyone look down on you because you are young, but set an example for the believers in speech, in life, in love, in faith and in purity.

—1 TIMOTHY 4:12

0   1   2   3   4   5   6   7   8   9   10

10. I am working with God to overcome my weaknesses.

If you are pleased with me, teach me your ways so I may know you and continue to find favor with you.

—EXODUS 33:13

0   1   2   3   4   5   6   7   8   9   10

D. Caring (Ministry)

1. I have discovered my spiritual gifts.

Therefore you do not lack any spiritual gift as you eagerly wait for our Lord Jesus Christ to be revealed.

—1 CORINTHIANS 1:7

0   1   2   3   4   5   6   7   8   9   10

2. I have an active ministry.

The King will reply, "I tell you the truth, whatever you did for one of the least of these brothers of mine, you did for me."

—MATTHEW 25:40

0   1   2   3   4   5   6   7   8   9   10

3. I am concerned about those who are in need.

   But a Samaritan, as he traveled, came where the man was; and when he saw him, he took pity on him.

   —LUKE 10:33

   0   1   2   3   4   5   6   7   8   9   10

4. I pray for those who are in need.

   We always thank God, the Father of our Lord Jesus Christ, when we pray for you.

   —COLOSSIANS 1:3

   0   1   2   3   4   5   6   7   8   9   10

5. I actively seek ways to help those who are in need.

   For I was hungry and you gave me something to eat, I was thirsty and you gave me something to drink, I was a stranger and you invited me in, I needed clothes and you clothed me, I was sick and you looked after me, I was in prison and you came to visit me.

   —MATTHEW 25:35–36

   0   1   2   3   4   5   6   7   8   9   10

6. I give my tithe to assist in God's kingdom work.

   "Bring the whole tithe into the storehouse, that there may be food in my house. Test me in this," says the LORD Almighty, "and see if I will not throw open the floodgates of heaven and pour out so much blessing that you will not have room enough for it."

   —MALACHI 3:10

   0   1   2   3   4   5   6   7   8   9   10

7. I pray for those who are in church leadership.

Pray for us. We are sure that we have a clear con-
science and desire to live honorably in every way.
—HEBREWS 13:18

0 1 2 3 4 5 6 7 8 9 10

8. I serve others even when it is not convenient.

You, my brothers, were called to be free. But do
not use your freedom to indulge the sinful nature;
rather, serve one another in love.
—GALATIANS 5:13

0 1 2 3 4 5 6 7 8 9 10

9. I make sacrifices of time to meet the needs of others.

Be imitators of God, therefore, as dearly loved children and live a life of love, just as Christ loved us
and gave himself up for us as a fragrant offering
and sacrifice to God.
—EPHESIANS 5:1–2

0 1 2 3 4 5 6 7 8 9 10

10. I am kind to strangers.

I was a stranger and you invited me in.
—MATTHEW 25:35

0 1 2 3 4 5 6 7 8 9 10

PLOTTING MY SCORE

Look at the graph below. You will notice that it has four quad-
rants, each one representing the four focus areas of the spiritual assessment. Ten circles from the inside to the outside
represent the 0 to 10 measurement for each question. Each
quadrant has ten lines, which are numbered and correspond

to question numbers on the assessments. If you answered the first question under the focus area of love with the number 7, you would make a dot where the seventh circle intersects the line numbered "1" in the "Loving" quadrant. Use this method to plot all of your answers.

The Spider Graph

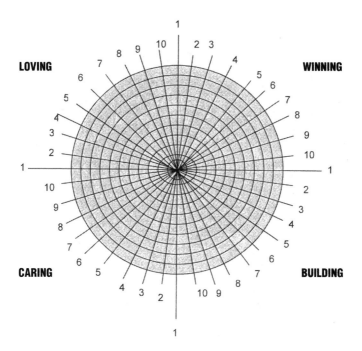

After you have plotted your answers, connect the dots. The lines will form what looks like a spider's web. Color the area from the center of the chart to the connecting lines, and this will reveal your spiritual strengths and weaknesses. Colored areas that extend close to the outside circle are areas of strength. Areas where there is little color are areas of weakness.

NOTES

1
THE PROPER MIND-SET

1. David Guralnik, *Webster's New World Dictionary* (New York: Simon & Schuster Publishing, 1982), 345.

2. Philip Yancey and Dr. Paul Brand, *In the Likeness of God* (Grand Rapids, MI: Zondervan, 2004), 35.

3. Yancey, *In the Likeness of God*, 36.

4. Ibid., 35–40.

2
THE PASSION

1. Rebecca St. James, *Sister Freaks* (New York: Warner Faith, 2006), 3.

2. Erwin Raphael McManus, *An Unstoppable Force: Daring to Become the Church God Had in Mind* (Loveland, CO: Group Publishing, 2001), 14.

3. Bob George, *Classic Christianity* (Eugene, OR: Harvest House Publishers, 1989), 58.

4. Larry Crabb, *The Pressure's Off* (Colorado Springs, CO: WaterBrook Press, 2002), 12.

5. Ibid.

6. Richard Foster, *Celebration of Discipline* (New York: HarperCollins, 1998), 33.

7. George Barna, *Grow Your Church From the Inside In* (Ventura, CA: Regal Books, 2002), 147.

8. Jim Herrington, Mike Bonem, and James Furr, *Leading Congregational Change: A Practical Guide for the Transformational Journey* (San Francisco, CA: Jossey-Bass Publishing, 2000), 34.

9. Ibid., 100.

10. John Kotter, *Leading Change* (Boston: Harvard Business School Press, 1996), 36.

11. Scott M. Boren, *Making Cell Groups Work: Navigating the Transformation to a Cell-Based Church* (Houston: Cell Group Resources, 2002), 89.

12. Kotter, *Leading Change*, 21.

3
THE PURPOSE

1. Rick Warren, *The Purpose Driven Church: Growth Without Compromising Your Message & Mission* (Grand Rapids, MI: Zondervan Publishing House, 1995), 42.

2. Ibid., 94.

3. Alan Nelson and Gene Appel, *How to Change Your Church Without Killing It* (Nashville: W Publishing Group, 2000) 53–58.

4. McManus, *An Unstoppable Force,* 190.

5. Warren, *The Purpose Driven Church,* 86.

6. Ibid., 87.

7. McManus, *An Unstoppable Force,* 67.

8. Ibid.

9. Ibid.

10. Ibid., 87.

11. Ibid.

12. Ibid., 112.

13. Warren, *The Purpose Driven Church,* 91.

14. Ibid.

15. Pat MacMillan, *The Performance Factor: Unlocking the Secrets of Teamwork* (Nashville, TN: Broadman & Holman Publishers, 2001), 44.

16. Ibid., 45.

17. Ibid., 46.

18. Boren, *Making Cell Groups Work,* 327.

19. Warren, *The Purpose Driven Church,* 93.

20. Ibid.

21. Gene Mims, *The Kingdom Focused Church: A Compelling Image of an Achievable Future* (Nashville, TN: Broadman and Holman Publishers, 2003), 76.

22. Ibid., 79.

23. Ibid., 81.

24. Ibid., 83.

25. Ibid., 85.

4
THE PLAN

1. Guralnik, *Webster's New World Dictionary,* 570.

2. William Bridges, *Managing Transitions: Making the Most of Change* (New York: Perseus Books, 1991), 52–59.

3. Warren, *The Purpose Driven Church,* 130–134.

4. Mims, *The Kingdom Focused Church,* 118.

5. Ibid., 113.

6. Ibid.

7. Ibid., 150.

8. Ken Hemphill and Bill Taylor, *Ten Best Practices to Make Your Sunday School Work* (Nashville: LifeWay Press, 2001), 13.

9. Barna, *Grow Your Church From the Inside In,* 122.

6
THE PARTICIPATION

1. Barna, *Grow Your Church From the Inside In,* 15.

7
THE PERSON

1. John Maxwell, *Winning With People* (Nashville, TN: Nelson Books, 2004), 20.

2. Daniel Goleman, "Leadership That Gets Results," Harvard Business Review (March–April, 2001), 78.

3. Ibid., 82–83.

4. Barna, *Grow Your Church From the Inside In,* 57.

5. Goleman, "Leadership That Gets Results," 80.

6. Ibid., 78.

7. Ibid., 80.

8. Ibid.

9. Ibid.

10, Ibid.

11. Guralnik, *Webster's New World Dictionary*, 110.

12. Ibid., 275.

13. Ibid., 802.

8
THE PROCESS

1. Dan Southerland, *Transitioning: Leading Your Church through Change* (Grand Rapids: Zondervan Publishing House, 2000), 56.

2. Larry Stockstill, *The Cell Church* (Ventura, CA: Regal Books, 1998), 101.

3. Joel Comiskey, *Groups 12: A New Way to Mobilize Leaders and Multiply Groups in Your Church* (Houston: Touch Publications, 1999), 135.

4. Dale Galloway, *The Small Group Book: The Practical Guide for Nurturing Christians and Building Churches* (Grand Rapids: Fleming H. Revell, 1995), 23.

9
THE PARTNERSHIP

1. Arthur W. Pink, *Gleanings From Paul: The Prayers of the Apostle* (Chicago: Moody Press, 1967), 154.

2. Dale Moody, *The Broadman Bible Commentary: Acts–1 Corinthians* (Nashville: Broadman Press, 1970), 253.

3. MacMillan, *The Performance Factor*, 26.

4. Ibid., 27.

5. Theresa Kline, *Remaking Teams: The Revolutionary Research-Based Guide That Puts Theory Into Practice* (San Francisco: Jossey-Bass, 1999), 8–9.

6. Ibid., 9.

7. MacMillan, *The Performance Factor*, 45.

8. Ibid., 46–47.

9. Ibid., 36.

10. Ibid., 35.

11. Randy Frazee, *The Connecting Church: Beyond Small Groups to Authentic Community* (Grand Rapids: Zondervan, 2001), 119.

12. Ed Young, *The 10 Commandments of Marriage: The Do's and Don'ts for a Lifelong Covenant* (Chicago: Moody Publishers, 2003), 214.

13. Mims, *The Kingdom Focused Church*, 16.

14. MacMillan, *The Performance Factor*, 35.

15. Ibid., 72–73.

16. Ibid., 36.

17. Ibid., 102–105.

18. Ibid., 37.

19. Ibid.

20. Ibid., 38.

21. Patrick Lencioni, *The Five Dysfunctions of a Team* (San Francisco: Jossey-Bass, 2002), 188.

22. Ibid.

23. Ibid.

24. Ibid., 189.

25. Ibid.

26. Ibid.

10
THE PROGRAM

1. Irma S. Rombaur, Marion Rombaur Becker, and Ethan Becker, *Joy of Cooking* (New York: Simon & Schuster, 1997), 110.

SELECTED BIBLIOGRAPHY

Allen, Diogenes. *Love: Christian Romance, Marriage, Friendship.* Cambridge: Cowley Publications, 1987.

Astin, Howard. *Body and Cell.* Grand Rapids: Monarch Books, 2002.

Barker, Steve, Judy Johnson, Rob Malone, Ron Nicholas, and Doug Whallon. *Good Things Come in Small Groups: The Dynamics of Good Group Life.* Downers Grove, IL: Inter Varsity Press, 1985.

Barna, George. *Grow Your Church From the Inside In.* Ventura, CA: Regal Books, 2002.

Barna, George. *Evangelism that Works: How to Reach Changing Generations with the Unchanging Gospel.* Ventura, CA: Regal Books, 1995.

_____. *Growing Your Church from the Inside In.* Ventura, CA: Regal Books, 2002.

Barnes, Richard, and Allen Jackson. *Teaching Youth: Leaders, Lessons, and Lifestyles.* Nashville: LifeWay Press, 2000.

Biech, Elaine. *The Pfeiffer Book of Successful Team-Building Tools.* San Francisco: Jossey-Bass/Pfeiffer Publishers, 2001.

Blackaby, Henry, and Richard Blackaby. *Spiritual Leadership: Moving People on to God's Agenda.* Nashville: Broadman & Holman Publishers, 2001.

Blanchard, Ken, Bill Hybels, and Phil Hodges. *Leadership by the Book: Tools to Transform Your Workplace.* New York: Waterbrook Press, 1999.

Boren, Scott M., and Don Tillman. *Cell Group Leader Training: Leadership Foundations for Groups that Work.* Houston: Cell Group Resources, 2002.

Boren, Scott M. "Church Focus: Bethany World Prayer Center, Baton Rouge, LA." *Cell Church Magazine.* Spring 1994.

Boren, Scott M. *Making Cell Groups Work: Navigating the Transformation to a Cell-Based Church.* Houston: Cell Group Resources, 2002.

Bridges, William. *Managing Transitions: Making the Most of Change.* New York: Perseus Books, 1991.

Caldwell, Max L. *A Guide to Standard Sunday School Work.* Nashville: Convention Press, 1982.

Callahan, Kennon L. *Twelve Keys to an Effective Church.* San Francisco: Harper and Row Publishers, 1983.

Carrier, Wallace H. *Teaching Adults in Sunday School.* Nashville: Convention Press, 1976.

Cladis, George. *Leading the Team-Based Church: How Pastors and Church Staffs Can Grow Together into a Powerful Fellowship of Leaders.* San Francisco: Jossey-Bass Publishers, 1999.

Comiskey, Joel. *Groups 12: A New Way to Mobilize Leaders and Multiply Groups in Your Church.* Houston: Touch Publications, 1999.

Crabb, Larry. *The Pressure's Off.* Colorado Springs, CO: WaterBrook Press, 2002.

_____. *Home Cell Group Explosion: How Your Small Group Can Grow and Multiply.* Houston: Touch Publications, 1998.

_____. "Six Habits of a Healthy Cell Leader." *Cell Church Magazine.* Fall 1998.

Dodge, Richard E., and Rick Edwards. *Adult Sunday School for a New Century.* Nashville: LifeWay Press, 1999.

Duck, Jeanie Daniel. *The Change Monster: The Human Forces That Fuel or Foil Corporate Transformation and Change.* New York: Three Rivers Press, 2001.

Earley, Dave. *8 Habits of Effective Small Group Leaders: Transforming Your Ministry Outside the Cell Meeting.* Houston: Cell Group Resources, 2001.

Eastman, Brett, Dee Eastman, Todd Wendorff, Denise Wendorff, and Karen Lee-Thorp. *Connecting with God's Family: Six Sessions on Fellowship.* Grand Rapids: Zondervan Publishing, 2002.

Edwards, Rick. *Teaching Adults: A Guide for Transformational Teaching.* Nashville: LifeWay Press, 2000.

Egli, Jim. "The Myth of the Instant Cell Church." *Cell Church Magazine.* Winter 1994.

_____. "The Ten Commandments of Transitioning." *Cell Church Magazine.* Fall 1996.

Element K Journals, Incorporated. *Power Point 2000 Computer Based Training.* CD-ROM. Available from www.elementkjournals.com.

Finzel, Hans. *Empowered Leaders: The Ten Principles of Christian Leadership.* Nashville: Word Publishing, 1998.

Firebaugh, Jay. "The Key is the Coach." *Cell Church Magazine.* Fall 1999.

Florida Baptist Convention Statistical Information. "Ten Year Church Profile: Woodland Baptist Church." *Church Information on Disc, 1993-2002.* CD-ROM, Florida Baptist Convention Resources, April, 2003.

Foster, Richard. *Celebration of Discipline.* New York: HarperCollins, 1998.

Frazee, Randy. *The Connecting Church: Beyond Small Groups to*

Authentic Community. Grand Rapids: Zondervan, 2001.

Galloway, Dale E. *20/20 Vision: How to Create a Successful Church with Lay Pastors and Cell Groups*. West Linn, OR: Scott Publishing, 1986.

George, Bob. *Classical Christianity*. Eugene, OR: Harvest House Publishers, 1989.

George, Carl, Paul Borthwick, Steve Sheeley, Paul Kaak, Carol Lukens, and Gary Newton. *Small Group Ministry*. Loveland, CO: Vital Ministry Books, 1999.

Gregory, John Milton. *The Seven Laws of Teaching: Revised Edition*. Grand Rapids: Baker Books, 1995.

Goleman, Daniel. "Leadership that Gets Results." *Harvard Business Review*. March–April 2001.

Goleman, Daniel, Richard Boyatzis, and Annie McKee. *Primal Leadership: Realizing the Power of Emotional Intelligence*. Boston, MA: Harvard Business School Press, 2002.

Gorman, Julie A. *Community That is Christian: A Handbook on Small Groups*, 2nd ed. Grand Rapids: Baker Books, 2002.

Guralnik, David. *Webster's New World Dictionary*, New York: Simon & Schuster, 1982.

Gustitus, Paul. *Destination Cell Church: Keys to a Successful Transition*. Ephrata, PA: House to House Publications, 2000.

Hadidian, Allen. *Discipleship: Helping Other Christians Grow*. Chicago: Moody Press, 1987.

Haggard, Ted. *Dog Training, Fly Fishing, and Sharing Christ in the 21st Century*. Nashville: Thomas Nelson, 2002.

Hargrave, James, and David Morrow. *Children's Sunday School for a New Century*. Nashville: LifeWay Press, 1999.

Hawkins, John. *Leadership as a Lifestyle: The Path to Personal Integrity and Positive Influence*. Provo, UT: Executive Excellence Publishing, 2001.

Hemphill, Ken, and Bill Taylor. *Ten Best Practices to Make Your Sunday School Work*. Nashville: LifeWay Press, 2001.

Herring, Jerri, and Larry Garner. *Five Handles for Getting a Grip on Your Sunday School*. Nashville: Broadman, 1997.

Herrington, Jim, Mike Bonem, and James Furr. *Leading Congregational Change: A Practical Guide for the Transformational Journey*. San Francisco: Jossey-Bass Publishing, 2000.

Hornsby, Billy. *The Cell-Driven Church: Bringing in the Harvest*. Mansfield, PA: Kingdom Publishing, 2000.

Honeycutt, Roy L., Jr. *The Broadman Bible Commentary: Exodus*. Nashville: Broadman Press, 1969.

Huey, F. B., Jr. *New American Commentary: Jeremiah, Lamentations.* Nashville: Broadman Press, 1993.

Hughes, R. Kent. *Acts: The Church Afire.* Wheaton: Crossway Books, 1996.

Hunter, Patrick E. "Developing a Group Ministry to Assimilate Both Prospects and Inactive Members into Active Membership in the Sunday School of First Baptist Church of Jacksonville, Arkansas." *D. Min. Project Report.* New Orleans Baptist Theological Seminary, 1996.

Hybels, Bill. *Courageous Leadership.* Grand Rapids: Zondervan Publishing, 2002.

Johnson, Douglas W. *The Care and Feeding of Volunteers.* Nashville, TN: Parthenon Press, 1978.

Johnson, Spencer. *Who Moved My Cheese?* New York: G. P. Putnam's Sons, 1998.

Johnston, Jay, and Ronald K. Brown. *Teaching the Jesus Way: Building a Transformational Teaching Ministry.* Nashville: LifeWay Press, 2000.

Jones, Samuel Ray Jr. "The Establishment of Home Bible Fellowship Units to Facilitate Church Growth at First Baptist Church, Birmingham, Alabama." *D. Min. Project Report.* New Orleans Baptist Theological Seminary, 1979.

Jordan, Ferris C. *Today's Adults: A Profile for Teachers and Leaders.* Nashville: Convention Press, 1993.

Kirkpatrick, Thomas G. *Small Groups in the Church: A Handbook for Creating Community.* New York: Alban Institute Publication, 1995.

Khong, Lawrence. *The Apostolic Cell Church: Practical Strategies for Growth and Outreach.* Singapore: Touch Ministries Publications, 2000.

Kline, Theresa. *Remaking Teams: The Revolutionary Research-Based Guide That Puts Theory Into Practice.* San Francisco: Jossey-Bass, 1999.

Kotter, John. *Leading Change.* Boston: Harvard Business School Press, 1996.

Lea, Thomas D., Griffin, Hayne P., Jr., *The New American Commentary: 1, 2 Timothy; Titus.* Nashville: Broadman Press, 1992.

Lewis, Frank. *The Team Builder: A Pastor's Resource for Increased Effectiveness in Developing and Leading the Church Staff.* Nashville, TN: Convention Press, 1997.

Lewis, Phillip V. *Transformational Leadership: A New Model for Total Church Involvement.* Nashville, TN: Broadman & Holman Publishing, Inc., 1996.

Lencioni, Patrick. *The Five Dysfunctions of a Team*. San Francisco: Jossey-Bass, 2002.

MacMillan, Pat. *The Performance Factor: Unlocking the Secrets of Teamwork*. Nashville, TN: Broadman & Holman Publishers, 2001.

Martin, Glen, and Gary McIntosh. *The Issachar Factor: Understanding Trends that Confront Your Church and Designing a Strategy for Success*. Nashville: Broadman & Holman Publishers, 1993.

Maxwell, John, *Winning With People*. Nashville: Nelson Books, 2004.

Mayer, Hal. *Step by Step: Transitioning Your Sunday School to Small Groups*. Littleton, CO: Serendipity House, 2001.

McBride, Neal F. *How to Build a Small Groups Ministry*. Colorado Springs: NavPress, 1995.

_____. *How to Lead Small Groups*. Colorado Springs: NavPress, 1990.

McManus, Erwin Raphael. *An Unstoppable Force: Daring to Become the Church God Had in Mind*. Loveland, CO: Group Publishing, 2001.

McAnally, Bryan. *The Servant Principle: Finding Fulfillment Through Obedience to Christ*. Nashville: Broadman & Holman Publishers, 1999.

McNeal, Reggie. *A Work of Heart: Understanding How God Shapes Spiritual Leaders*. San Francisco: Jossey-Bass Publishers, 2000.

Mims, Gene. *The Kingdom Focused Church: A Compelling Image of an Achievable Future*. Nashville: Broadman and Holman Publishers, 2003.

Minnery, Tom. *Why You Can't Stay Silent: A Biblical Mandate to Shape Our Culture*. Wheaton, IL: Tyndale House Publishers, Inc., 2001.

Moody, Dale. *The Broadman Bible Commentary:Acts–1 Corinthians*. Nashville: Broadman Press, 1970.

Murren, Doug. *Leadershift: How to Lead Your Church into the 21st Century by Managing Change*. Ventura, CA: Regal Books, 1994.

Nanus, Burt. *Visionary Leadership*. San Francisco: Jossey-Bass, 1992.

Neighbour, Ralph W., Jr. *Where Do We Go from Here?: A Guidebook for the Cell Group Church*. Houston: Touch Publications, Inc., 1990.

_____. "Structuring Your Church for Growth – An Examination of Three Cell Structures." *Cell Church Magazine*. Summer 1998.

_____. "Transitioning." *Cell Church Magazine*. Fall 1995.

Nelson, Alan, and Gene Appel. *How to Change Your Church Without Killing It*. Nashville: W Publishing Group, 2000.

Pink, Arthur W. *Gleanings From Paul: The Prayers of the Apostle*. Chicago: Moody Press, 1967.

Polhill, John B. *The New American Commentary: Acts*. Nashville:

Broadman Press, 1992.

Rainer, Thomas. *High Expectations: The Remarkable Secret for Keeping People in Your Church*. Nashville: Broadman & Holman Publishers, 1999.

Ramage, James Michael. "Developing a Program of Relational Evangelism Through Home Cell Units as a Ministry of West St. Charles Baptist Church, Boutte, Louisiana." *D. Min. Project Report*. New Orleans Baptist Theological Seminary, 1991.

Raughton, Alan, and Louis Hanks. *Essentials for Excellence: Connecting Sunday School to Life*. Nashville: LifeWay Church Resources, 2003.

Red Bull Divide and Conquer Race. Internet Site. http://www .redbulldivideandconquer.com/results.php.

Reid, Clyde. *Groups Alive—Church Alive: The Effective Use of Small Groups in the Local Church*. New York: Harper and Row Publishers, 1969.

Rees, Jeff. "Transitioning: The 'Transitionally-Challenged' Love 'em or Leave 'em." *Cell Church Magazine*. Fall 1996.

Richards, Lawrence O. *A Practical Theology of Spirituality*. Grand Rapids: Zondervan Publishing House, 1987.

Riley, Joseph C. "Developing a Ministering Church by Small Group Training at St. Joseph Baptist Church, St. Joseph, Louisiana." *D. Min. Project Report*. New Orleans Baptist Theological Seminary, 1978.

Rombaur, Irma S., Marion Rombaur Becker, Ethan Becker. *Joy of Cooking*. New York: Simon & Schuster, 1997.

Sauder, Brian, and Larry Kreider. *Helping You Build Cell Churches: A Comprehensive Training Manual for Pastors, Cell Leaders, and Church Planters*. Ephrata, PA: House to House Publications, 2000.

Schultz, Thom, and Joani Shultz. *The Dirt on Learning: Groundbreaking Tools to Grow Faith in Youth Church*. Loveland: Group Publishing, 1999.

Senge, Peter M. *The Fifth Discipline: The Art and Practice of the Learning Organization*. New York: Doubleday Publishing, 1990.

Sharkey, Ricky Allen. "Developing a Small-Group Leadership Training Program at Celebration Church, Metairie, Louisiana." *D. Min. Project Report*. New Orleans Baptist Theological Seminary, 1997.

Smith, Jack R. *Friends Forever: Studies in Relational Evangelism*. Nashville: Convention Press, 1994.

Southerland, Dan. *Transitioning: Leading Your Church through Change*. Grand Rapids: Zondervan, 2000.

Stafford, Tim. "Finding God in Small Groups." *Christianity Today.* August 2003.

Stanley, Andy. *Visioneering: God's Blueprint for Developing and Maintaining Personal Vision.* Sisters, OR: Multnomah Publishers, 1999.

Stockstill, Larry. *The Cell Church.* Ventura, CA: Regal Books, 1998.

Sweet, Leonard. *Aqua Church: Essential Leadership Arts for Piloting Your Church in Today's Fluid Culture.* Loveland, CO: Group Publishing, 1999.

_____. *Post-Modern Pilgrims: First Century Passion for the 21st Century World.* Nashville: Broadman & Holman Publishers, 2000.

Swenson, Richard A. *Margin.* Colorado Springs: NavPress Publishing Group, 1992.

The Abringer Institute. *Leadership and Self-Deception: Getting Out of the Box.* San Francisco: Berrett-Koehler Publishers, Inc., 2002.

Wagner, Peter C. *Home Cell Group Explosion: How Your Small Group Can Grow and Multiply.* Houston: Touch Publications, 1998.

Warren, Rick. *The Purpose Driven Church: Growth Without Compromising Your Message & Mission.* Grand Rapids: Zondervan, 1995.

Welch, Bobby H. *Evangelism Through the Sunday School: A Journey of Faith.* Nashville: Lifeway Press, 1997.

Wiersbe, Warren W. *Be Basic: Believing the Simple Truth of God's Word.* Colorado Springs: Chariot Victor Publishing, 1998.

_____. *Wiersbe's Expository Outlines on the New Testament.* Wheaton: Victor Books, 1992.

Wilkes, Gene. C. *Jesus on Leadership: Discovering the Secrets of Servant Leadership from the Life of Christ.* Wheaton: Tyndale House Publishing, Inc., 1998.

Wilkinson, Bruce. *The 7 Laws of the Learner: How to Teach Almost Anything to Practically Anyone.* Atlanta: Walk Through the Bible Ministries, Inc. Publishers, 1988.

Wren, J. Thomas. *The Leader's Companion: Insights on Leadership Through the Ages.* New York: The Free Press, 1995.

Wuthnow, Robert. "How Small Groups Are Transforming Our Lives." *Christianity Today.* February 7, 1994.

Yonggi Cho, Paul. *Successful Home Cell Groups.* South Plainfield, NJ, 1981.

Yount, William R. *Created to Learn: A Christian Teacher's Introduction to Educational Psychology.* Nashville: Broadman and Holman Publishers, 1996.